What People Are Saying

*The Journey To Competitive Advantage Through...*

A thought provoking and insightful look into the often underestimated and misunderstood field of leadership in business; Bill Flint's The Journey To Competitive Advantage Through Servant Leadership offers a pragmatic "Golden Rule" guide to being a responsible and inspiring leader. A "must read" book for professional and personal enlightenment in what it takes to bring out the best in your people and yourself.

> **Dr. Stormy T. W. Hicks, Ph.D.,** Former President & COO of J.B. Poindexter Co., and ITT Automotive, and Executive Director of Ford Motor Company

Bill takes real life experiences and learning's to teach us about people-centered leadership. He presents compelling anecdotes and logic to demonstrate what it is, how to do it right and why effective "servant leadership" is the master key that unlocks success with any team, business, or organization. Bill's values, principles, passion, successes, and "lessons learned" shine through and provide a didactic roadmap for aspiring leaders.

> **Bruce Freeman**, Operating Partner, Thompson Street Capital Partners

Bill Flint has achieved considerable success in an impressive business career, but he is also one of those all-to-rare individuals who have graced the business world with a life of faith and principle. This book compiles the lessons of a lifetime into one comprehensive document that can help point the way for future leaders to the fulfilling life of what some call "servant leadership" - that powerful, almost mystical capability to help people achieve beyond their fondest dreams, while living a life of faith and making priceless contributions to their family, the community and the greater world.

> **John Beakes**, President, Operational Performance Solutions, Inc.

The Journey To Competitive Advantage Through Servant Leadership is packed with life lessons that can greatly improve your life and your business. Bill Flint takes a highly ethical and moral approach to developing employees, running your business, and balancing your life. He provides practical examples of how to build a business of which you can be proud and where employees can excel. The wisdom of treating others like you want to be treated rather than how you have been treated raises the bar in employee relations. Helping people succeed and achieve their goals is a time proven way to ensure that you too will succeed. Everyone can benefit from the lessons that Bill has learned from his successes and challenges. If you are seeking to improve your career, be a leader in all you do, build a business of integrity, or balance your life with better relationships with family and friends - this book is for you!

**Dennis J. Hocker, PhD**, Co-Founder of The Coach Academy

Reading The Journey To Competitive Advantage Through Servant Leadership is like listening to the author speak. Anyone who knows Bill Flint treasures time with him and knows that it was time well spent. Some books are read and shelved, while others are read, reread and loaned to others. This is the latter. Some books are outdated within months of their release…born of the wisdom of humanity, while others have a timeless quality born from the heart of God. This is the latter. It offers truths that saturate the heart and life of Bill Flint…truths that have guided great men and women for thousands of years. Profitable for teaching, correcting and training there is fodder for staff meetings, newsletters and training seminars on every page. If a reader is looking for platitudes and/or original theoretical possibilities look elsewhere. This is a hands on, get the job done and done right guide for blue collar management. It will feed the best parts of you.

**David M. Hutchens**, Senior Pastor, Walnut Hill Bible Church, Baraboo, Wisconsin

There's no better place to learn high level leadership than from someone that's done it on the front lines. Bill has taken his vast years of experience, his direct teaching approach and put it all together in The Journey To Competitive Advantage Through Servant Leadership. It will raise your level of leadership by heeding Bill's coaching and putting these principles into practice

**Dave Engbrecht**, Senior Pastor, Nappanee Missionary Church, Nappanee, Indiana

# The Journey To Competitive Advantage Through Servant Leadership

Building The Company Every Person Dreams Of Working For And Every President Has A Vision Of Leading

Bill B. Flint Jr.

WESTBOW
PRESS
A DIVISION OF THOMAS NELSON

WestBow Press books may be ordered through booksellers or by contacting:

WestBow Press
A Division of Thomas Nelson
1663 Liberty Drive
Bloomington, IN 47403
www.westbowpress.com
1-(866) 928-1240

ISBN: 978-1-4497-3196-0 (sc)
ISBN: 978-1-4497-3198-4 (hc)
ISBN: 978-1-4497-3197-7 (e)

Library of Congress Control Number: 2011960656

Printed in the United States of America

WestBow Press rev. date: 11/28/2011

# DEDICATION

To my wife, Kay, who has given me unconditional love, encouragement, and lots of grace during our journey together.

To my sons, Andy and Patrick. I have been blessed being your dad, and you have brought me great joy and happiness.

To Jesi, my awesome daughter-in-law, who is like a daughter to both Kay and I, and to Will and Sam, my two grandsons, for their love and the awesome hugs they give to "Pop Pops."

Last, but not least, to my parents, Bill and Iretta Flint who have gone to be with the Lord. They taught me so much about servant leadership, being a good parent, and making a marriage last by working to put God first in your life. It was a privilege and blessing to be their son.

The most valuable "currency" of any organization is the initiative and creativity of its members. Every leader has the solemn moral responsibility to develop these to the maximum in all his people. This is the leader's highest priority." W. Edwards Deming, in *Principle-Centered Leadership.*

# Contents

# Introduction

Can you imagine the excitement people would feel coming to work every day to a company where leaders understood that building a sustainable competitive advantage for the organization is based on how people are treated and developed by their leaders? A company where leaders view people as their most important asset, and they are not just words in a mission statement. Where leaders recognize their workforce comes to work bringing their dreams, goals, skills, and potential for achieving something bigger than themselves, and the role of leadership is to help their people discover and reach their potential. So, what type of leadership is needed to make this type of business culture a reality?

I believe what is needed are trained Servant Leaders: *men and women who bring their purpose, passion, and character, and when combined with their God-given skills and abilities for leadership, bring out the best in people, helping a business develop and implement a sustainable process for success.*

This is accomplished because servant leaders discovered during their life's journey their purpose, which is a genuine caring for people, and it is then combined with their passion for leading people in a business setting. This purpose and passion, along with their leadership skills and talents, helps create a business atmosphere of shared vision, values, and accountability for the results.

*The Journey To Competitive Advantage Through Servant Leadership* was written to help leaders and businesses take an honest look at their current leadership skills and styles, the need and advantage of developing servant leaders and their leadership principles, and to help companies maximize the potential of their people, therefore, creating a sustainable competitive advantage for them and security for their people.

If we take that honest look, we will see that our current stress filled and unpredictable economic condition and the selfish focus many leaders have developed are creating a crisis in leadership around the world. Because of this crisis I believe servant leadership training, principles and skills are the answer to help us:

- Restore the loss of trust and respect that people feel for their leaders.
- Develop a new collaborative relationship between leadership and the people they lead to help develop relationships that provides security for both the people and organization.
- Emphasize relationship building by teaching leaders how to lead to make a difference in their people's lives, by helping those they lead discover and develop their full potential.
- Eliminate the stress and frustrations many leaders feel today, because they feel inadequate in leading their people. Not because leaders are bad people or don't want to do a good job as a leader, but because companies are not providing the continuous training, coaching, and mentoring leaders need to succeed.

When most people are first promoted into a leadership position, it usually has very little to do with their ability to lead people. They were promoted because they were good at tasks. They were a good salesperson, good at fixing machines, a good engineer, and good with numbers, or a family member. So what we have done is throw first-time leaders "into a lion's pit" with no weapons. These new leaders have had little to no training, and the ongoing training at many companies is only a couple days a year at best, and maybe a few sessions with the person they report to. It's not because companies don't care; it's because they are trying to find the time to provide training, develop training on a limited budget, and make it a priority while dealing with the "daily fire drills" of the business.

In business, we love to use sports analogies in our discussions, but we seem to forget that the greatest athletes in the world spend a tremendous amount of time each day training to improve their skills. They know it's key to improving. But many leaders spend very little time working to improve their own leadership skills and don't provide the training needed to improve the skills of the people they ask to achieve continuous improvement year after year. Then, we wonder why our people turnover is high, the people and leaders are stressed and frustrated with each other, and the gap between our goals and actual results is growing wider and wider.

## MY BOOK WAS WRITTEN TO HELP YOU

- Understand how servant leadership principles, skills, and characteristics can help leaders have a positive impact on their people and company
- Learn from my own servant leadership journey, including the successes and struggles, and how I discovered my purpose and passion
- Build an environment of trust with the people you lead, which brings reliability, predictability, and accountability
- Learn how to discover and develop the unique and collective skills, abilities, and talents of your workforce
- Identify and remove the barriers that keep people from reaching their potential
- Understand the importance of improving communication and resolving conflict
- Identify the five leadership styles in every company and understand their impact on people and results
- Develop a culture where leaders help people become problem solvers
- Develop strategies to improve team building and relationships, creating an atmosphere of innovation and imagination
- Guide your organization in how to view servant leadership skill development as an ongoing process of training, coaching, and mentoring, and if servant leadership principles are implemented and followed, they can produce maximum performance and results for the company and the people

# CHAPTER ONE

# WHO AND WHAT IS A SERVANT LEADER?

> Whoever wants to become great among you must be your
> servant, and whoever wants to be first must be slave of all.
> Mark 10:43–44 (NIV)

Rarely will you hear the term "servant leader" used when people refer to a leader in a business or see it listed on a company's organizational chart. Actually, when the two words "servant and leader" are used together, it often brings puzzled looks, because these two words seem like complete opposites. The word "servant" brings thoughts of a person who is weak and allows others to push him or her around, while the word "leader" brings visions of a person of strength, someone in charge and telling others what to do. However, when you combine these two words, it describes a leader who is anything but weak.

## MY DEFINITION OF A SERVANT LEADER IN A BUSINESS

*Men and women who bring their purpose, passion, and character, and when combined with their God-given skills and abilities for leadership, bring out the best in people, helping a business develop and implement a sustainable process for success.*

They discovered during their life's journey their purpose, which is a genuine caring for people. It is then combined with their passion for leading people in a business setting. This purpose and passion, along with their leadership skills and talents, help create a business atmosphere of shared vision, values, and accountability for the results.

I will share how a servant leader's principles, skills, vision, philosophy, and strategy guide him or her, how it can make a difference in a company's results, and why companies should make it a priority to develop a training process for developing servant leaders and establish servant leadership as a goal for their leaders.

My book is based on what I have learned during my thirty-eight-year business career in the manufacturing sector; with twenty-five of those years in senior leadership positions I held in privately held, family-owned, public, mid-sized, and two Fortune 500 companies. While I have learned much during my own leadership journey, I also learned by watching many other leaders, both good and bad, and the impact their actions and decisions had on people and their companies. The goal, theme, and prayer for my book is to help leaders and organizations understand it is truly possible to **build the company every person dreams of working for and every president has a vision of leading.**

A workplace that is possible if authentic servant leaders are in place, and their principles for leading and serving are supported and allowed to flourish and grow within a business. Servant leaders bring a focus that is about impacting people's lives by doing the right things for the right reasons. It is a unique style of leadership that helps companies develop and nurture the unique and collective skills, abilities, and talents of the people within their company. Servant leaders believe the best way to develop a successful company is by caring for and focusing on the people who come to work each day and help them discover and reach their potential.

I believe seeing leadership as your competitive advantage is important, because in most businesses, your competitors can buy or rent a building, purchase the same equipment and raw materials, produce the same products or services, and chase the same customers and markets you do. What is hard for your competitors to duplicate is a servant leadership team that realizes its awesome responsibility of caring for, leading, and impacting the lives of people, while at the same time serving as stewards of the business, its resources, and the results. It is a unique balancing act that many leaders have the talent to bring but have not yet discovered this purpose or developed the passion of caring for people that servant leadership requires. They may have been hindered by their own personal motives, what they were taught by other leaders, their inability to overcome the pull of selfishness we all deal with, or the lack of training and coaching needed to help them discover their own leadership purpose and skills.

## SERVANT LEADERS UNDERSTAND

- That people come to work every day with their unique personalities, dreams, goals, skills, and hunger for achieving something bigger than themselves. What they need is the right style of leadership, communication, training, and guidance to help them reach their potential. People don't come to work to fail, produce bad products and services, or have a bad day. It is a leader's responsibility to lead them by teaching, encouraging, and helping them find and reach their potential. That is what leaders with a purpose and passion for people are called to do.
- They need to paint a picture, so to speak, to help people understand what needs to be accomplished and why. Then, they need to motivate, encourage, inspire, and support their people in ways that bring them together to accomplish company goals and objectives. It's about concentrating on the people who do the blocking and tackling every day.
- Because they have discovered their purpose is to make a difference in the lives of the people God places in their path, they work to build an atmosphere of unity and community within the business where they serve and lead.

I know when I talk to some people in business about the need for building a sense of community in the workplace, they will show some skepticism. But if you think of it in these simple terms, maybe it will help.

- We spend more of our time (when we are awake) with the people we work with; more time than we spend with our own families.
- People need relationships in their life.
- People want to feel good about accomplishing something of value.

So, we can either create an environment where people are encouraged, motivated, and feel part of something bigger than themselves, or treat them like labor (I don't like that word) and watch them go home every day frustrated and miserable. In which environment would you choose to work? Which do you believe will produce the best results over time? How would the people in your company answer?

I feel this subject is so important to the business world that becoming a servant leader should become the goal of every individual who has been called to be a leader, and the goal of every company should be to make it a priority to train, teach, nurture, and develop servant leaders who can positively influence people in a way that truly makes a difference in people's lives.

I know making the statement, "being called to be a leader," can create debate over whether leaders are born or developed. In my humble opinion, after thirty-eight years in business, I am convinced true leaders are born and have been blessed by God with the purpose, passion, talents, skills, and potential needed to become a servant leader.

You will notice in the last paragraph I used the words "potential needed" to become a servant leader. Why? Because it is a lifelong journey of development and growth, similar to those who are born with natural athletic ability but need to develop those skills to achieve athletic success. When my children were younger, I coached soccer and baseball for young children, and I could easily spot those born with athletic ability. They had a rhythm and skill level that other young children struggled with. But to continue developing those skills as they grow and mature requires practice, training, coaching, and continued work to improve and fine-tune their skills. Those blessed with leadership skills and talents must go through that same maturing, training, studying, and life journey to become a servant leader. It doesn't happen overnight or by someone waving a magic wand. Both servant leadership and competitive advantage are built by building a consistent process that is developed over time through both positive experiences and the struggles they will face.

**Lesson Learned: Servant leaders are not developed by accident or without a process, plan, purpose, and passion.**

## HOW TO RECOGNIZE A SERVANT LEADER

Servant leaders can be identified by their actions, words, and sacrifice. They are recognized by the way their people are working and achieving as individuals and as a team. One important thought about servant leaders: they don't need a title. You will find servant leaders in many companies working behind the scenes without ever receiving an official title as a leader, but who have a major impact and influence on the people with whom they work. People go to these unofficial leaders, because they have earned their trust by their behavior, ability, and character. Just having a title doesn't bring a lot of value when it comes to leading. Being a true leader has to do with who has influence and has built trust by their actions—a trust built moment by moment, over time, through both good and challenging times. As the old saying goes, "All leaders have influence; is it positive or negative?"

One of the first clues for discovering a servant leader is listening for how they talk about those they lead. When I hear leaders talk about how dumb or lazy their people are or how their people don't get it, my ears perk up. It tells me people are not important to those leaders, or the leaders don't understand their role in caring for people and helping them reach their potential. I have been in many meetings during my career and heard leaders discuss how people can easily be replaced. When the door is closed and people talk in private is when you can tell how they really feel. Their real voice will be heard.

However, while servant leaders can and do get frustrated with their people, if they discuss their people and their issues, it will not be in a public setting or group. Talking about how people need to change or improve in their job is normal and different than talking about a person or a group in a way that puts them down and doesn't show respect for the individual. Never make it personal about the individual; make it about the performance if something needs to be improved or corrected. There will always be people in any company who create issues, stir up things, and need to change their behavior. But even then, they deserve respect and need to be treated fairly, even if disciplined or terminated.

Servant leaders make it a priority to help each individual they lead to improve and grow in their skills, abilities, and job. Servant leaders work hard to remove the barriers that get in the way of people reaching their potential. They work to create an environment where each individual sees their role and responsibility for helping make the group and company stronger.

## HOW IS SERVANT LEADERSHIP DEVELOPED?

As I stated earlier, I believe true leaders are gifted at birth with potential, but to become a servant leader requires their skills and abilities to be nurtured, tested, and developed through the many experiences they encounter during their life and leadership journey.

One way it's gained is by watching and listening to other leaders to see the impact their leadership skills and styles have on people. I can look back on my own leadership journey and see some of the best lessons I learned were by watching inadequate leaders who didn't have a clue about leadership. I saw how people felt, how it demoralized the workforce, and how the results of the business suffered. I saw how people tried to hide when they saw that leader coming. They dreaded even talking to that leader or being around him or her. I watched people lie and hide results, because they didn't want to feel the wrath of their leader. The biggest issues in business today are not caused by competitors or the economy. They are caused by poor leaders and leaders who have the potential but have not been trained. These issues are:

- Poor communication that creates most of the other issues businesses struggle with every day
- People treated poorly by leaders who don't see the people who actually do the work as their most important priority
- Businesses and their leaders that know what the issues and challenge are but do not work together to solve them, leaving everyone frustrated and alienated from each other
- Conflict that is allowed to go unresolved and just festers and creates lots of stress and frustration for everyone

Personally, I was very blessed to have many good mentor leaders who poured their time and life into me and the others they led. They weren't perfect—no servant leader is—but they knew their own weaknesses, they were humble, they listened to other people's ideas, and when things weren't going well, they were on the front lines, talking with people and not hiding in their office. They took the blame themselves and gave credit to others for accomplishing the results. They were always teaching, communicating, and looking for ways to help everyone feel good about their efforts, what they were working toward, and celebrating even small successes.

**Lesson Learned: To become a better leader requires a personal commitment to keep growing as a leader** by reading leadership books, attending training sessions and seminars on leadership, even if your company doesn't pay for them. Servant leaders learn to invest in their own future; they know it isn't just the company's responsibility. On many occasions, I bought my own books and paid to attend seminars I thought would help me become a better leader. Servant leaders know they need to keep growing as a leader.

Developing as a servant leader is also about being in the game, learning through trial and error during your leadership journey. It's about learning, growing, and becoming aware of your weaknesses, what causes your frustrations, taking chances by reaching out to people who are difficult to work with, and by setting and reaching stretch goals. They know it's harder to learn sitting on the sidelines, and getting some bruises from time to time is how you learn.

I can look back over my own career and see that when I got my first promotion to regional sales manager at age twenty-eight, I wasn't really prepared. I was asked to move from Charlotte, North Carolina, to Atlanta, Georgia, to open a regional office for our company. For me, it was about the title, the excitement of the move, the money, and how proud it made me feel. Thinking about impacting and helping people reach their goals and full potential wasn't really on my radar. Oh, I cared about people; I was considered a nice guy, but I didn't see my promotion as some high purpose or calling to impact people's lives. I got the promotion because I was a good salesperson. I received no training and was thrown into the leadership role with a pat on the back and a "go get-em" speech. I remember telling the three salespeople who reported to me to call me once a week, mail me their weekly reports (no e-mail back then), and if I needed them, I would call. And, if they were asked, to be sure to always tell the boss that I was doing a great job. Now, that must have really made them feel real secure with me as their leader. I thought it was all about me.

It wasn't until I was thirty-nine years old and was promoted to sales and marketing manager for a division of a Fortune 500 company that

I started realizing that if I could help others succeed and took the focus off my wants, ego, and accomplishments, I could accomplish a lot more. Luckily, I had some very experienced manufacturer's reps that had been sales managers during their careers take me under their wings. They taught me that being a sales and marketing manager was about spending time with them, making sure they had the resources to be successful, taking care of our customers, and if I did all that right, it would help me become successful. That is when my leadership role started to come alive for me.

**Lesson Learned: Work to help your people become successful and you will do well and so will the company.** Those lessons started me on my servant leadership journey, along with my relationship journey with God, which I will write about later.

## PEOPLE WILL IMPACT YOUR JOURNEY

When I think about my own journey, I can see the faces of so many people who sacrificed their time and effort to help me move forward. It started with God, who gave me the skills, talents, and opportunities with which I was blessed. My wife poured her love into me and our children and made sacrifices so I could spend many nights away from home, traveling on business, staying late at work or out with customers and salespeople. I believe most servant leaders—man or woman—have someone who has been key in teaching them about service, sacrifice, love, and support.

**Lesson Learned: Spouses are major contributors to the success of most servant leaders.** The sad part is I took my wife's sacrifice for granted for many years. I didn't appreciate her sacrifices like I should have. I'm thankful that God finally woke me up to how much she means to me and the importance of her sacrifice to me and my life's journey.

**Lesson Learned: Success is never won on your own; there are many partners.** I really appreciate the leaders who didn't kill or fire me when I made mistakes that cost the company money or time. I remember the leaders who spent their time teaching and coaching me when I made the wrong decisions or how I should look at something in a new or a different way. I appreciate the great pastors who taught me about giving grace and mercy to the people God put in my life. If I wanted grace and mercy, I needed to give it to others. There are also the several thousand people I had the privilege of working with and leading during my career, who really did the work that made me look good and taught me so much about leadership and what is important to people. Without their patience and support of me as a leader, I could have easily gone down the wrong path as a leader. I am forever grateful.

## KEY LESSONS LEARNED DURING MY JOURNEY

- People don't come to work to have a bad day or do a poor job.
- People are important and should not be treated like some nameless individual.
- The people in any business are very smart, and leaders need to listen.
- Most issues in business are due to a lack of communication.
- Real change in a business starts with leadership standing shoulder to shoulder with their people, not issuing e-mails, memos, or a one-time "we need to change" speech. Change is a journey not an event.
- The diversity of the people in a business brings strength, not weakness.
- When we allow problems to go too long, the workforce feels leadership must not care, so it must not be important.
- Supervisors and middle managers have a tremendous amount of influence. Most need more training and coaching.
- Too much time is spent telling people what is wrong and not enough time looking for what is right.
- Feedback is important, because people want to know how they are doing.
- Problems are opportunities. Use them as teachable moments.
- Most companies don't spend enough time training their people. Real training is not about giving out information; it's about making a difference and bringing about change.
- A positive attitude is infectious.
- Give people a way for their ideas, suggestions, and concerns to be heard.
- The more time and sacrifice I made for my team, the more they give back. I could not out give them.

Early on in my career, I had a leader pull me aside and tell me how I was showing selfishness in the way I was leading my people and dealing with my peers. He taught me ***the pull of selfishness is strong on a leader***, and we must always be on guard and quickly notice the selfishness when it starts. The first time you look in the mirror and start telling yourself how much smarter and brighter you are than your peers, or your department is better than all the others and you are worthy of the success you have attained, you need to sound the alarm and do something quickly to put out that "dangerous fire."

Servant leaders can waste their skills and abilities when they are corrupted by allowing selfishness, greed, and desire for power drive their leadership motives. These are things that can easily result in poor results and failure both for the leader and the organization. One of hardest things for any leader is working to keep selfishness and the dreaded, "It's all about me," syndrome from taking you down the wrong leadership path. I have seen it many times in leaders with whom I have worked. Usually, it's when the big, new title or raise comes, and people start singing praises about how smart you are or how you turned around the company or department. You begin thinking you did it all by yourself, and the others rode your back and couldn't have done it without you.

## CONGRESS: EXAMPLE OF LEADERSHIP GONE BAD

As I am writing this book, I'm saddened to see our congressional leaders fight over budgets, the debt ceiling, taxes, and so many other subjects. It makes my head spin. What is sad is that I do not see many servant leaders in Congress. It doesn't matter whether they are Democrats, Republicans, or Independents. Their decisions seem to be driven by how it makes them and their party look, getting reelected, making the other political party look bad, and stretching the truth to make if fit their beliefs. The finger-pointing is almost unbearable. If they just knew, or maybe better yet really cared, how bad it made them and us as a country look; maybe they would work to change. But they seem to talk in doublespeak, so they never have to give a straight answer. Then, if they do talk, all they do is blame the other party. Real leaders never blame others.

Servant leaders sit down and try to resolve conflict. They wouldn't keep stoking the fire with their words of conflict and name-calling. They would talk in private, not air the dirty laundry on TV and radio. They wouldn't try and always one-up the other leaders. They would find ways to compromise, so everyone can get a little credit for the win. Servant leaders don't call other people names, and they do what is right for those they lead. One thing I have noticed about those in Congress, they almost always refer to each other as the Republicans or Democrats when speaking about each other. They talk like they are all opponents instead of a team of servant leaders working together to solve our country's problems.

Servant leaders would see each of their fellow congresspersons as an individual who has ideas. Even though they might be different, they would show respect and, more important, they would remember that little rule that says, "Every person in any argument has a little piece of right." If we had servant leaders, our halls of Congress would be filled with voices of respect and humble attitudes, and leaders would do the right thing in the right way for the right purpose. Now we seem to have a group of adults, acting like children arguing on the playground. I apologize to children everywhere for comparing you to our Congress. I know a servant leader shouldn't talk like this, but it felt good to write it. Please forgive me this one time. I couldn't help myself.

## A SERVANT LEADER

What makes a servant leader different? Do they have the same desires for their life and inner drive to succeed as other leaders? What fuels their passion? Do they judge success differently? What is their purpose?

Servant leaders come in all sizes, ages, genders, and nationalities. They work in small and large companies, both private and public. They have different personalities and styles, but their values, vision, and calling are similar.

## SERVANT LEADERS CAN BE IDENTIFIED BY

- How they treat people with respect
- Their positive attitude
- A desire to serve others
- The time they spend with their team
- Their communication and conflict resolution skills

- More one-on-one meetings with their people
- Giving and seeking feedback from their direct reports, peers, and their own leaders
- Their ability to handle bad news and not panic
- The respect people show them
- Their influence with people
- Their motivation to serve to make a difference in people's lives
- By the high standard they hold themselves and their team
- By the way they care for people

**Lesson Learned: While some leaders have a tendency to value certain people more than others, servant leaders believe no single person is more important than another.**

Obviously, servant leaders are human, and there may be people they like to be around a little more because of that person's actions or personality. But you will not see them play favorites with their people. Everyone is equal as a person in a servant leader's eyes. Now, that doesn't mean people with certain skills won't get promoted or given training to help them grow. But that kind of treatment is open to anyone who has the ability or skills to move forward. Servant leaders understand that it's the diversity of the workforce that is vital to the success of the organization. They see the diversity as strength, where other leaders might see people's differences as a weakness. Those types of leaders want everyone to conform to their ideas and see how things should be only through the eyes of the leader. That style puts people in a box, with little motivation or chance to break out.

**Lesson Learned: Servant leaders also believe that a workforce and team are successful because of their dependence on each other for the success of the group.** They believe that each person is gifted with certain talents and skills, and the coming together of those unique differences creates the opportunity for greater success for the organization. They believe that if a diverse workforce is led correctly and their unique differences cultivated, a highly functioning organization can be developed. If not led correctly, the group can become dysfunctional and will not reach their own potential and the desired goals and objectives set for the group or the company.

## COLLEGE FOOTBALL EXAMPLE OF LEADERSHIP AND DIVERSITY

In business, we love talking about sports and often use sports teams as examples for leadership and team building. If we really understood the leadership dynamics that take place with successful coaches and how they handle leadership and diversity, we would copy many of their techniques for leading a diverse workforce. Football coaches recruit highly competitive young men right out of high school from all over the country. They come with different backgrounds, skill sets, expectations, maturity levels, abilities, and attitudes. There are some sixty to ninety players who must come together to form a team. All the team members must play together and give their best for the team to succeed.

The coaches develop a plan on how to turn these young men into a team, in spite of the fact the players are competing against each other for a spot as a starter. They practice each day, hitting each other as hard as they can during practice to win a starting position. They eat, study, and spend time together, all while competing against each other and getting ready to do battle against their real competitors: other teams. Somehow, what sounds like dysfunction works. They remain a team, even after some become starters and others must take a backseat and still support those who just beat them out for a starting position.

How can coaches accomplish this? The ones who accomplish this on a consistent basis are able to do so because they create the right organization, motivation, encouragement, education, expectations, communication, accountability, and energy to pour into these kids. A defined, deliberate, proactive strategy and discipline are all part of a strategy to create winners by helping them discover and develop their potential and become winners. The coaches yell (even cuss at times), make players run extra laps, and create a much-disciplined environment, with lots of rules and punishment if not followed. Poor attitudes and big egos are not allowed. So, how does it work in spite of the tough environment and the competition? It's because these young football players know their coaches care and are sacrificing and pouring themselves and time into their lives to help them become not only better football players but also better men. They are helping them reach their potential, using all the servant leadership skills you read about earlier in this chapter. It's felt and shown every day to the players. Ask yourself, if it can work for a football team, why can't it work in business?

13

Now, I'm not promoting that we all start blocking and tackling each other in the parking lot, on the factory floor, or in the office, or we wear pads and helmets to work. But what if we could duplicate that caring, disciplined team approach and process as servant leaders in our own organizations? There is no telling what we might accomplish in the lives of people and the results of our organizations. Now, let's go suit up, and get ready for the game. But, no tackling!

# CHAPTER TWO

# THE SERVANT LEADER DIFFERENCE

### Servant Leaders Bring A Vision That Believes

The best strategy to achieve organizational goals and create competitive advantage is by developing an environment of caring, mutual trust, and respect between the leaders and the people by focusing their efforts and strategy on developing the full potential of all associates and the business, therefore creating a winning partnership.

## SERVANT LEADERS LIVE THEIR VISION BY

- Treating people as the *most important asset* in the company
- Seeing people not as they are today but *their potential*
- Realizing people are *more important than tasks*
- Measuring their own success by *the success of those they lead*
- Knowing leadership is *about building relationships* throughout the company
- Impacting people's lives *by mentoring and coaching*
- Setting *goals, objectives, actions, and measurements with accountability for the results*
- Leading not just with their words but *with their actions and modeling the behavior*
- Believing it is the responsibility of leaders to *make a difference in people's lives*
- *Encouraging, inspiring, and motivating their people*

## SERVANT LEADERS HELP PEOPLE

- Learn to trust, which brings reliability, predictability, and accountability
- Feel a part of something bigger than themselves
- Implement discipline and hold themselves accountable for their actions and results
- Take initiative to make it better than when they arrived
- Learn how they can help improve the company and themselves
- Feel part of a team
- Learn the importance of communication and resolving conflict
- Appreciate the diversity of the workforce
- Create a learning and innovative climate
- Harness their collective potential to maximize their results

## THE WRONG PEOPLE CAN END UP IN LEADERSHIP

One of the important lessons I learned shortly after being named president of a company headquartered in Wisconsin is that people can and do end up in leadership positions who shouldn't. I learned this valuable lesson as I held meetings with the production supervisors at each of our facilities in North America to talk about my expectations for them and my leadership philosophy. But as I got further into these meetings, one theme kept coming up over and over again. Many of the supervisors were not happy in their jobs. They had been promoted years earlier, because they had been good at maintenance or setup techs. They were good at doing technical tasks. That was their skill and first love. Yet, when the chance to be promoted came up, they jumped at the opportunity, because it was more money, they thought they would be happier, and a title came with it. Most people don't really understand the toll leadership takes on them and their family until they get into a position of leadership. It always looks good on the outside looking in. It looks glamorous, and people see money and power.

But these supervisors quickly found out that leadership is not as easy as it looks. They learned they didn't like dealing with people issues, which meant their teams were not getting the attention needed, and issues and problems were not quickly resolved or handled. Plus, with our best maintenance and setup techs now promoted into leadership, we were seeing maintenance

16

issues and longer setup times than we had previously experienced. So, I made the decision to put several of them back into their old jobs at the same pay rate they were receiving as supervisors, hired or promoted more-experienced supervisors, and implemented training for supervisors and team leaders.

**Lesson Learned: Don't promote people just because they want to make more money or you are afraid you will lose them if they aren't promoted**.

Train candidates first to determine if they have leadership skills or keep them in their current positions if they are that good, and pay them more money. That way, everyone wins. In talking to other leaders, I know many companies struggle with this same issue. It's the Peter Principle in action.

I have learned that the wrong move in promoting a person into leadership can demoralize a whole department, and you can lose a good person who was doing an excellent job in their previous role. And you now have to hire or promote another person, who might create a worse situation. I know companies have pay grades to worry about, but we should not become slaves to pay grades. We have to use good common sense and judgment. Think not just about the short-term but also the long-term impact of promoting someone.

## BEFORE PROMOTING SOMEONE YOU NEED TO

- List five main reasons why you think the person will be a good leader.
- Ask what leadership experience or traits the individual has.
- Understand the main issues and challenges of the department or group he or she will be leading today and in the next three years.
- Determine if his or her background, experience, and skill level fits those needs.
- Seek the opinion of others who have worked with anyone you are considering promoting.
- Take your time. Don't rush just because you have an opening, and you want to fill it quickly.
- Use personality, skills, motivators, and abilities tests to determine if someone is suited for leadership.

- Remember leadership is about leading people, not tasks.
- Have more than one candidate for an open position. Don't limit your thinking or options.

One question I learned to ask people I was considering for a promotion is, "If you could stay in your current position and make the same money you would if promoted, would you take the promotion or stay in your current position, and why? But you must be prepared to pay that person that salary if he or she decides to stay in the current position.

## WHEN LEADERS FALL

I believe the more successful and powerful you become (the world's view of success), the more difficult it becomes to remain the person who started out on that journey of servant leadership. The battlefield is littered with fallen business, spiritual, and political leaders, who started out with the right motives but let selfishness take control of their lives. They start reading their own press and believing it was by their hand and might they found the keys to success. Success can become like a drug, and you can't get enough. You lose control and look for the next high or the next great thing to make you feel like you own the world, that no one or anything can stop you. It becomes all about you, your power, your needs, your desires to do anything you want. **Lesson Learned: Leaders fall because of selfishness and belief in their own strength.**

As I wrote earlier, I believe selfishness is the number-one reason leaders fall. They put themselves first, while servant leaders work to put others first. Selfishness is a danger to all leaders. As a servant leader, it is something you will always have to guard against. You will not be immune. Why, because as a servant leader, many people will want your time and attention. Some will want it because of very legitimate reasons; others will want to gain something from you. Their selfishness will drive the need for your time. You will be popular as a servant leader because of the way you treat people and your success as a leader. People will be attracted to someone who treats them fairly and with respect. You may start to feel worthy of all the praise and attention, instead of feeling thankful for the blessings God has provided to you through the skills, abilities, and opportunities he has provided. **Lesson Learned: Be on guard against feeling important and starting to love that feeling of importance.**

## MAIN REASONS LEADERS FALL

- Money, fortune, and fame become their number-one goal, instead of making a difference in people's lives.
- They love the attention from people who are always trying to gain their favor (kissing up).
- Looking good becomes more important than doing good.
- It becomes about them and their success.
- They quit holding themselves accountable.
- They are able to filter out the truth.
- They lose their moral compass as to what is right and wrong.
- People who were once important to them are now just objects to help them gain what they want.
- Even their families become less important than they used to be.
- They start making excuses for their behavior.
- Last but not least, their relationship with God has become less important to them.

## SERVANT LEADERS NEED TO UNDERSTAND THEMSELVES

- You are not perfect and will make mistakes.
- You will have to fight off the same temptations that most everyone goes through.
- You will get frustrated when you struggle for the right solutions to problems.
- You need mentors and coaches to hold you accountable.
- You will sometimes hire the wrong people and go to long before terminating people who shouldn't have been hired.
- You will sometimes doubt yourself.
- You will get down on yourself.
- You have weaknesses, but you will recognize many of them.
- You will not be liked by everyone.
- You will not get through to everyone you lead.
- You will wonder if you are too easy on people at times.
- You will ask yourself if it is worth the sacrifice.
- You will struggle and have challenges.
- You will get off track at times with your family.
- You will have your faith tested over and over again.

But you will survive if you keep your priorities on track. Most servant leaders I have met or worked with in my life had an inner strength, peace, and wisdom that many never understand. True servant leaders understand the strength, wisdom, talents, and skills they have comes not from anything they have created but from God, who has chosen to bless them so they can impact the lives of the people he brings into their lives. True servant leaders have found their purpose in life, and it is serving in a way that has a lasting and positive impact on the lives of the people God puts in their path.

Leadership is a high calling. It's one filled with opportunity and failure. You will sometimes wonder if it's worth it. In spite of your best efforts in your job, there will be circumstances beyond your control, and you will miss the mark. But if you are called to be a servant leader, be the best you can be. Keep looking in that mirror to see if you are still that person who is humbled by the chance to lead and are still passionate about caring for and leading people. If you ever see yourself becoming a person who believes he or she has arrived, has all the answers, and it's all about you, quickly get on your knees and pray for wisdom, guidance, and a new direction. **Lesson Learned: Remember that our priorities determine our decisions, our decisions will determine our paths, and our paths will determine our journey.**

**Lesson Learned: Don't ever forget your greatest calling as a leader is your family.** Don't ever devote so much time and effort that you don't have the energy or time to serve and love your family. Don't fool yourself into believing that all the hours away from home are so you can give your family all the things they deserve. It will do you no good to build a great company full of happy people and a large bank account for yourself and watch your family slip away or be destroyed. Learn to balance the leadership of your family, your associates, and your company.

There are two old sayings that my dad used to tell me when I was growing up: (1) when someone is near death, you never hear the person say, "I wish I had spent more time at the office." The other one was, (2) "When a person dies, you never see a funeral hearse pulling a U-Haul, because you can't take your money and possessions with you." Remember these sayings when you are struggling with the right priorities in your life.

# CHAPTER THREE

# THE FIVE LEADERSHIP STYLES

In this chapter, we examine the five leadership styles I have encountered during my business career. Each style impacts people and a business in different ways. Some styles will help a business and its people improve, while others keep them from achieving their goals and can actually inflict harm on people and the business, both now and in the future.

Most leaders are not bad people, and many would love to have the training, coaching, and mentoring needed to become the leader they want and need to become. However, there are some leaders who just don't get it, and if they read my descriptions of the different styles of leadership in this chapter, they won't recognize themselves. They are blind to the negative impact they have on people, their own weaknesses, and how they are hurting the company's results. These types of leaders usually blame others for both their and the company's failures. Along their leadership journey, they got caught up in the selfish mode, and it has taken them far away from the original leadership path.

Having too many styles of leadership in a company has the potential to create confusion and frustration for the people working there. These differences can also keep the leadership team from coming together because of the differences in their values, thought processes, and how they view people. From my own experience, I can say without a doubt that not all leaders see people as their most important asset. I have been in meetings when leaders have said things that leaders of people should never let leave their lips.

Differences in leadership styles or the wrong styles can also create issues when the leadership team tries to develop and implement their vision and strategy for the company. While they may all agree in a private conference room on the direction of the company, when the rubber meets the road with real-life actions, they won't support it. This happens when each leader takes the vision and strategy message back to their departments or teams and puts his or her own spin on the message based on personal beliefs and style, causing confusion and misunderstanding among the workforce. **Lesson Learned: Servant leaders believe when you have any important message, especially those that have to do with vision, values, expectations, strategy or bad news, you must deliver that message yourself so you can ensure the right message has been given and is understood**. Servant leaders also believe these types of messages must always be given in person and not through some e-mail, memo, or bulletin board message. You can follow up with something in writing, but the initial message must be in person.

Obviously, some businesses can find some success having a mix of leadership styles, because many have. But if you have too many of the wrong styles, it can create major issues, unnecessary stress, organizational issues, and challenges for the company's leadership. The more aligned leaders are in their values, style, and views on how to lead people, the more likely they are to work together and find success. If leadership is not aligned correctly, their days will be filled with conflict and stress, while success comes and goes like the wind. **Lesson Learned: The type and mix of leadership styles will make a difference in a company's results.**

The success of a business can also be negatively impacted if senior leadership is focused on the idea people, "are our most important asset," and middle management and team leaders aren't on that same page. The message that senior leadership wants delivered will be watered down and presented the way middle management perceives it or wants the people to hear it. This will confuse the workforce, and they will keep asking why leadership doesn't see all the issues and problems. Senior leadership will get the blame for how people are being treated. **Lesson Learned: To keep this from happening, senior leadership needs to keep communication open and often with the workforce, so they don't get all their information from**

**middle management**, who usually has less experience in leading, may have the wrong leadership style, or has very little leadership ability, because training programs are weak or nonexistent. Knowing the capabilities of your middle management and supervisors is a must for any leadership team.

## YOU CAN BE AMBUSHED BY MIDDLE MANAGEMENT

The following example happened during a town meeting I was holding as president to introduce a new communication improvement program for our company. After the meeting, I noticed one of the supervisors pull one of the machine operators off to the side. This operator had asked some very good questions during the meeting that pointed to issues that were not being handled correctly. My experience told me the supervisor was not going to thank her for asking tough questions; he was going to tell her to never ever do that again. Sure enough, that is what I heard. So, I made this a teachable moment for everyone.

Sometimes moments like this present themselves, and a leader must take advantage. They are the best kind of teaching moments, because people can see you take on another leader who has said or done the wrong thing and handle it right on the spot. I told everyone to sit back down, and I asked the supervisor what he was talking to the operator about. The room got so quiet you could have heard a pin drop. He gave me the answer I expected: "Nothing." I asked the operator what the supervisor had discussed with her, and, of course, she didn't want to answer. So, I told them what I heard. I made a very strong point that this was not to ever happen again, because I was very serious about our need to improve the way we communicate and for every team member to feel they had the right and responsibility to bring their ideas and concerns out in the open and to us as leaders. I told the group that if our leaders couldn't live up to my vision that people were important and needed to be treated as such, I would help them find another career. Pretty tough talk for me, but it had to be done at that moment. A line in the sand had to be drawn.

As you can imagine, it didn't take long for everyone on every shift to hear about this meeting and how I stood up for the people. It made me a hero, as this was only my third week as president at this company. But when you take a stand like this, you have to back it up with more than words. It must be followed up with consistent action, and it cannot just be a one-time event and expected to stick. People will keep testing you to see what you are made of and if you would go back to your office, like many before me, and not ever mention it again. This company was a very special situation. I was the fourth president in three years, so you can imagine how confused the people had become and the lack of expectations and discipline that existed.

We had many more moments like this, with changes made in supervision and leadership that were required to move the company forward. This same scene is played out in companies all over the country, day after day. In all honesty, I have allowed it to happen myself, going too long without replacing a leader with the wrong style and attitude who wouldn't change. There are several reasons why this scene happens in business:

- There are people who should have never been placed in a leadership position.
- Most companies know who their poor leaders are, but they move slowly or not at all in working with them to improve or remove them for their poor leadership.
- As leaders, we feel we can turn around a bad manager or leader, so we keep trying and go way too long before making a change.
- Many companies do not provide the investment in money and time for the consistent and effective training needed for both new and seasoned leaders. Skills need to be developed if we want to put feet to our vision that people are our most important asset. If we really want to impact people's lives, build a trust between leadership and the associates, and see our results improve, it won't happen by letting leaders mistreat, ignore, and make our people feel like second-class citizens.

## THE FIVE LEADERSHIP STYLES

1. Servant Leader
2. Potential Servant Leader
3. Passive Leader
4. Boss
5. Unofficial Leader

## 1. Servant Leader

I humbly believe that servant leaders have the potential to provide the most positive impact (over the long-term) on people and the results for any business. No, they are not perfect: they will make some wrong decisions, they will try to get things implemented that other leaders will not support, and they will be impacted by things they cannot control. But if leadership will allow them to do what is needed, great things can happen. However, what I have usually seen is that many companies have a hard time allowing servant leaders to make the changes needed. This lack of support is caused by old paradigms, preconceived notions of the past, and uncertainty about treating people with the strategies a servant leader brings. I know leaders who believe if you treat people too well, they will take advantage of you. They don't like to give compliments or celebrate too often, because they believe it will spoil people. It's this kind of thinking that causes many problems for servant leaders and companies.

The servant leader is the rarest of the five types of leaders you will find in a business. Not because there aren't many out there with the skills and abilities to become a servant leader but because:

- They may not know that being a servant leader is something they should aspire to be. If they don't know about the term or the skills and style that identify a servant leader, they won't know it's something they want to improve on or become.
- Businesses are not providing the training and focus needed to take leaders to the servant leadership level. Most businesses aren't discussing servant leadership or establishing it as a goal for their leadership. Most businesses haven't identified "servant leader" as a term to be used internally. It isn't talked about very often outside the church or nonprofit organizations. So, while leaders may be exhibiting the servant leader traits in their business, they have not been labeled as such or told this is a behavior the business wants to develop and duplicate within the company.

However, there is hope, as we are seeing more talk about ethics, morals, and servant leadership by colleges, universities, and fine non-profit organizations such as, The Greenleaf Center for Servant Leadership located in Westfield, Indiana. I believe this recognition for servant leadership is being driven by the many failures of leadership we are seeing in business, politics, banking, sports, and even in ministry. Newspapers and TV are filled almost every day with the failures of leaders with wrong motives. People are becoming less and less trustful of leaders. People are starting to recognize that a fall is coming—if not today, then tomorrow. Every leader deals with the pull of selfishness on their life. But servant leaders are able to overcome that pull, or at least control it, and not make the big mistakes that destroy their lives and those of others. As leaders, we need to talk more about how selfishness traps leaders, what success in life is really about, and when is enough, enough. **Lesson Learned: Selfish leadership brings hurt not just to the leader but to his or her family and the many lives a leader touches and impacts.**

### Servant Leaders Have A Heart For People

They believe that building caring relationships with the people they lead, and helping them to improve their skills and develop their full potential, is best for the people and the business. They believe if they can truly help people succeed, it is the best way to build a lasting, competitive advantage for the business and provides a great work environment, creating a true win-win for both the people and the company.

## MAIN CHARACTERISTICS OF A SERVANT LEADER

- Caring for and having a positive impact on people through their leadership is their purpose and passion
- Builds real relationships with people
- Open-minded, great communicator seeks and gives feedback, great listener
- Involved with their team
- Helpful
- Delegates to and empowers their people
- Manages and resolves conflict; sets goals and expectations
- Believes in accountability for the results
- Motivates and encourages; establishes a vision, so people understand their role
- Doesn't blame others
- Gives praise
- Constantly training their people, both one-on-one and in groups

- Team builder
- Role model for other leaders
- Aware and honest about their weaknesses
- Shows patience
- Serves with humility
- Their actions match their talk
- Willing to pay the price for building relationships
- God is usually the foundation for their life.

All leaders have and will exhibit some of these traits and skills at some point in their career—or at least some of the time. It may be to just a few favored people, or they force themselves for the wrong motives. But servant leaders are consistent in showing these characteristics and traits. It is a way of life for them. It comes naturally, is real, and is driven by their caring and desire to impact people's lives. Now, with that said, servant leaders do get off track from time to time. There are not perfect people: not even servant leaders. They have days their people exasperate them. They have days they wonder if anyone appreciates or cares about them. They want to do well for their families and yes, even themselves. But they have this great ability to fight through the selfish issues in their lives faster and better than most. They, "can play hurt," as one of my mentors used to say when describing leaders who could give their best in spite of how they felt or what was going on around them.

## 2. Potential Servant Leader

These are leaders who are starting to show servant leader skills and characteristics but have some more seasoning to go before reaching servant leader status. They need more experience leading people and going through the fire, so to speak. More than likely, they are younger or new to their leadership role. Remember: I said in chapter one that servant leadership is a journey that never stops and must be earned. Focusing on and truly caring for people as the way to success for the individual and the company must become a leader's passion and purpose, not just a slogan. Many in this category are at a crossroads as to the direction their leadership will take them. Their path will take them toward servant leadership, staying where they are, or moving into the other two types of leadership we will discuss. Their motives for leadership as they evolve and change (what is important to them in life) and their maturity level will be major factors as to which path they end take.

## CHARACTERISTICS OF POTENTIAL SERVANT LEADERS

- Seeks more responsibility; they like leading people
- Definitely has the servant leader skills and DNA, but they need to be developed
- Has big dreams for moving up the corporate ladder; needs to determine motives
- People enjoy being around them; they can be charismatic
- Are starting to care about people but maybe haven't discovered if that is their purpose
- Almost all servant leaders pass through this stage during their careers
- Very good people skills
- Motivates people but struggles with the purpose of the motivation. Is it to help them look good as a leader, or is it driven because they care for the people they lead?
- Very goal-oriented, but mostly for themselves at this stage
- Working on delegation but worries if they turn over work to others and they don't do a good job, it will make them look bad as the leader
- Can be helpful at times, but stays very busy with tasks
- Communicates, but sends way too many e-mails instead of communicating face to face and one-on-one with their direct reports
- Sets expectations but gets frustrated a little too much
- Empowers those they like but not everyone who reports to them
- Is working on conflict resolution skills; likes to win in discussions

This group needs servant leadership training to help them move down that path. Without it, they can easily stay in this category or move to the #4 type leader style.

Servant leaders love this kind of up-and-coming leader. Servant leaders will try hard to mentor and coach them. Many of these leaders will be grateful for the coaching, but some of those who choose other leadership paths will see servant leaders as competition and in their way of advancement. If you read this and feel you are in this category, remember my suggestion from chapter one, and look in the mirror often. Ask yourself, what are my motives? Do you need to rethink your path? If so, seek the help of a servant leader. He or she will be very happy to help you work through your questions, doubts, and confusion. That is what servant leaders do. One question to ask yourself as you evaluate where you are on your leadership path is, when people come to you for help or with questions, are you usually excited they seek you out and happy to help, or do you usually see it as an inconvenience, because they are taking up your valuable time? Your honest answer will give you a clue to where you are and on what you need to work.

The next two types of leaders can have a very negative impact on a business but in different ways. Both try and avoid each other at all costs. They are at opposite ends of the leadership chart.

## 3. The Passive Leader

People fall in this category for several reasons. They have given up on their career, have been passed over for promotions, have personal issues going on in their life, or they don't want to rock the boat. They are trying to hide and stay out of the way. They don't want to draw any attention to themselves unless it is an easy, no-brainer project.

## PASSIVE LEADER CHARACTERISTICS

- They allow important issues to go unresolved or are late getting them completed
- They avoid conflict at almost any cost
- They are usually likable
- Sometimes, they are just lazy, but that is not the usual case
- They have good ideas but not real sure of themselves
- Their people quit coming to them, because their suggestions and ideas go nowhere, and they rarely hear back
- They don't stand up for their people
- The leader they report to may be treating them badly or unfairly

- They don't have much vision for the future
- They are quiet in meetings
- They are afraid of rejection
- They would rather do things themselves than delegate

In their defense, there may be something going on in their personal life that is a distraction (example: marriage issues, sickness in the family or with themselves).

Many times, this person has passed the point where he or she can be salvaged as a leader who can have an impact on the business and people. But maybe they can be moved back to the potential servant leader style with some coaching and training, or if there has been a personal issue that has been resolved. The individual's leadership style is hurting the results of the company, but just as important, the people who report to this person are not being led. The individual is not reaching his or her full potential, and no one is helping that person improve his or her skills. The person feels the company doesn't care about him or her, and senior leadership gets the blame. This type of leadership exists in many companies and needs to be resolved quickly.

## 4. The Boss

This is a term you don't hear used in corporate America very much anymore. When I first entered the business world in the 1970s, it was a term you heard a lot. However, being called a "boss" today doesn't have a very endearing feel to it for a leader. It sounds like someone who doesn't really care about people. It is the old "demand and control" style of leadership People who fall into this category can have a very negative impact on a business. If a company really does care about its people, this type of leader does more to damage how people feel about the company than any other style. This style of leadership demoralizes the people who report to this style of leader and negatively impacts the company's results. It screams people are not important.

## BOSS CHARACTERISTICS
- They look at leadership as having power over people
- Titles are very important to them

- They believe they are always right
- They believe people can easily be replaced
- They believe training is a waste of time
- They give very little feedback and don't ask for any
- They communicate by telling people what to do
- They can be very emotional, especially if things are not going well
- They need to win arguments. If they lose, they pout or get even
- They believe they are smarter than anyone else in the room
- They have little patience working with difficult people
- People try to avoid them
- They can be charming when they want something
- They blame others for mistakes
- They spend very little time with their people

This leader is almost always a lost cause and usually needs to be let go if you really believe people are your most important asset. They are a poison to companies that want to improve their results and have an impact on people's lives.

The potential servant leader and passive leader styles need ongoing training, mentoring, and coaching programs to help them move forward. However, many companies do not have a very effective training program or strategy for developing leaders. Many HR departments are handcuffed by small budgets for training and follow-up coaching, so accountability for improving their leadership skills doesn't happen or isn't considered very important. This isn't because leaders don't care, but because they get busy working in the business and not on the business. They run out of time or the focus shifts to some other issues, and training is not seen as a high priority for improving results. If training does happen, it's something that takes place a couple days a year and is then forgotten, with no follow-up to keep those who need leadership development on track.

I want to repeat what I said in chapter one. If your company does not offer training for servant leadership or leadership improvement, you as an individual need to take responsibility and find good leadership training tools and pay for them yourself. As leaders, it's our responsibility to take steps to improve our leadership skills and abilities, so we can impact people and help improve our company's results. Accomplishing this may require you to find the time to take leadership classes, attend seminars, buy training tapes, and read some good leadership books. Take the steps needed to help you impact your people and company, and take your leadership skills to the next level.

## 5. Unofficial Leader

This leader's name will not be found listed on an organizational chart, because it is not recognized as an official leadership title. But they are recognized within the ranks of the workforce. They are usually people who have very good technical knowledge, common sense, listening skills, a heart for people, and a special knowledge of the company. They usually have been with the company for some time and are well liked and respected by most in the company. They can help smooth things over when people don't understand what is going on, or they can create some negative issues for leadership if they turn against leadership or don't like the way things are being managed in the company. You can find them in every company and department. Servant leader and potential servant leader styles usually work and communicate well with this group, because they understand the influence they have on people. The boss style doesn't work with this group and works to avoid and eliminate their influence.

I have worked with several of these types of people in the two manufacturing companies where I served as president. They were very helpful to me, and I could always count on them to give me an honest opinion on what we should or shouldn't be doing. I didn't always agree with them, but I wanted to know their thoughts and have a relationship with them. I also found that most of them didn't have any interest in becoming an official leader with a title. I think they liked having some influence, without the accountability for the results.

As we close out this chapter, I want to comment on the diversity and differences in people you find in every company. One thing I love most about business is that it takes all types of personalities, skills, and abilities to make a business work effectively. It truly is a community of people who come to work with different goals, ideas, and reasons for being there. It is the role of leadership to take all these unique people, their talents and skills, and figure out how to harness, develop, and lead this collective ability and potential. That is what leaders do.

If leadership can truly learn how to lead this diverse group, a business can achieve goals and results they never thought possible. But if leadership takes their eye off the ball and doesn't treat people with respect and the belief that people really are their most important asset, it can become a disaster and a miserable place for the people and leaders: a place where people just go through the motions and watch the clock, waiting for the workday to end. Then, they come back each day with a little less energy and eagerness to achieve great things.

Leaders set the pace and the rhythm of a business or organization. So, it is important that the right style of leadership is in place to achieve sustainable success. **Lesson Learned: Leaders always have influence; the question is whether it is the kind that impacts people's lives and the business in a positive and sustainable way. Or does it kill their innovativeness, ideas, passion, and enthusiasm for doing a good job?** The styles of leadership you allow to exist in your company, or the style of leader you aspire to become, does matter, and if you don't believe it, ask your people—if you can stand to hear the truth.

# CHAPTER FOUR

# DNA OF A SERVANT LEADER

As I stated earlier in the book, I believe certain people are born with the God- given skills, talents, and abilities needed to develop into a servant leader. Those skills can either be developed or wasted, depending on the paths they choose and the decisions they make during their life journey. Some people will find their purpose early in life, some may take longer, and others will miss it all together. I believe servant leadership is developed and nurtured as we move through life, developing our character and strengths, fighting through our weaknesses, determining our priorities, all moving us toward finding our passion and God's purpose for our lives. We are all designed for greatness by God. The question is where we look to find it and what we are willing to sacrifice during our journey to take hold of it.

In this chapter, I discuss what I believe to be part of every servant leader's DNA. It's what drives the servant leader to discover their purpose for impacting people's lives and to devote themselves and their careers to helping people and companies accomplish some amazing things while working together. It's what helps to hold a servant leader steady when life seems to be coming at him or her fast and furious.

So there is no confusion, I am not a psychologist, PhD, or researcher with any scientific proof for what I'm writing in this book. I'm sharing what I have learned, experienced, and observed in myself, and also the many leaders I have worked with during my business career. My knowledge and beliefs have also been impacted by working with and observing many servant leaders in churches and nonprofit organizations, who have made serving their lifelong career or as unpaid volunteers. My opinions and thoughts have also been developed by working with, leading, and listening to the many people who really get the work done each and every day in businesses throughout the country.

## SERVANT LEADERS' DNA

1. Relationship with God
2. Care About People
3. Stewardship
4. Communicator
5. Humble
6. Positive Attitude
7. Encourager
8. Motivator
9. Influencer
10. Accountability

## 1. Relationship With God (Discovering My Own Purpose)

While talking about God in business books is something some might discourage, I cannot write about servant leadership or my own journey of growing as a leader without including my relationship with God. I believe each of us has been created by God with a special purpose for our lives. Many of us will spend a lifetime trying to find that purpose and then work to develop and nurture it. God has equipped every person ever created with the skills, abilities, talents, and personality for that journey of discovering and fulfilling our purpose. Most of us will struggle to find that purpose. Or at least I did. I struggled, and still do, with what is important to me and the priorities for my life. I believe it's very important that we each search for and find the purpose God planned for us. **Lesson Learned: Finding God's purpose for our lives is what will bring us the real success, joy and happiness that we all seek.**

The struggle for me was trying to determine what real success and happiness looked like. When I was younger, like many before me, I thought success was about money, big cars, job titles, and accumulating stuff. As I mentioned in an earlier chapter, when I got my first leadership promotion, it was about the raise, the title, and looking good to my friends. It had nothing to do with people or the impact my leadership could have on those I led. It was all about me and what I wanted.

My first big encounter with finding my purpose came in 1986, at the age of thirty-six. I had just taken a new job with a division of a Fortune 500 company as product manager. Again, it was about the money, the new job title, and working for a big company. The only downside about taking this job was moving from Charlotte, North Carolina, to a much-smaller town in eastern North Carolina. Soon after moving, my wife and I started attending a small church, figuring not much would be going on, and we could hide. Boy, were we wrong. Soon after we started attending regularly, the pastor asked me to teach a vacation Bible school class of junior high boys and girls. I had never taught in church or to children, but I thought this would be easy, until I got the book they wanted me to teach: *Hormones in Tennis Shoes*. Well, I taught the class and was popular with the kids, because I told them more than I should. But the parents weren't happy with me, because I did tell them too much. But I survived and learned that I loved teaching, because you could get instant feedback from the people you were teaching.

A few months later, they asked me to teach the junior high Sunday school class permanently, and I said yes. I loved teaching, and for me—who never really liked school too much except for sports, hanging out with my friends, and being social—this was unusual. As for my job as product manager, that was going well, and I was starting to learn about helping people achieve their goals. I was promoted to sales and marketing manager for the company at age thirty-nine.

The light bulb was starting to come on for me, as I enjoyed teaching Sunday school more and more. I was now a deacon in the church, and my wife and I were responsible for the Sunday school department, teachers, and classes, which meant meetings, strategizing, and training along with deacon meetings.

I was enjoying training salespeople and helping them develop their territory strategies and reach their quotas. I gained more responsibility as sales and marketing manager, with customer service now reporting to me, along with fifteen sales reps and twelve distributors. My goals were becoming more about helping people succeed in their work and helping those we taught at church grow in their relationship with God and his son, Jesus Christ.

We were so happy. Our sons were seven and five. They were playing soccer (I was even coaching) and doing well in school. Our church was growing, Sunday school attendance had doubled, and we had a new pastor with a great vision. Work was going great, and life was good.

Then, God started stirring in 1991. I got a call from a company in Baraboo, Wisconsin, about an opening for vice president of sales and marketing. I visited that company, because my dad always taught me, "When God opens a door, go through it and then wait for God to close it or open it wide." This would be a big move, since we would be leaving all our friends and family in the South and would have to become "Cheeseheads" and "Badgers." Not only was that scary, but thinking about the cold and snow didn't make it easy. I had my doubts but kept talking with that company.

Long story short, I took the job after lots of prayer. My wife, Kay, made the decision we were going, because I couldn't make up my mind. Well, God was faithful and blessed our move in March 1991. I was blessed as vice president of sales and marketing with a great team of people and the family who owned the company was very supportive of my family and I. Kay and I started attending church right away at Walnut Hill Bible Church, and I began teaching the high school boys Sunday school class, and Kay taught young children. Then, a few years later, Kay and I started a young married Sunday school class, and we discovered our passion was teaching young married couples about how to deal with the struggles all married couples go through. Kay also became children's church director, and I served on the deacon board. We also became Sunday school directors. I served as building committee chairman, as our church grew, and we built a new church building. We added on again due to the growth and the many people God was sending to our church. God was truly blessing our family, church, new friendships and work.

God was keeping our plate full, but he was faithful to give us the time and energy to keep up with him, our two sons, and my work. Later in 1996, I was promoted to senior vice president at work and in 1998, was promoted to president of the company. We had grown the business to $125 million in annual sales by 2003, with 1100 associates, and ten facilities, including one in Mexico and one in England.

As president I enjoyed holding town meetings at all the facilities, creating a communications strategy to give all associates a voice. I developed and introduced training and leadership courses, which I taught before hiring a training director to keep the momentum going. **Lesson Learned: Our people have so much to teach us as leaders about what we are doing wrong and how they can help us fix it.** I enjoyed the new leaders I had put in place throughout the company. Being able to coach, mentor, and watch leaders grow and people pulling together really got me excited. Between church, work, and God working in my life, servant leadership was starting to make sense. I was finding that my passion and purpose was about impacting people's lives in a positive way, helping them deal with their struggles and reach their potential. I was really starting to care about people and how I could make a difference in their lives.

Life was great, but God starting stirring again, with an opportunity that came out of nowhere. This was hard to imagine, since we loved our church and were so excited that God was allowing us to be involved with so many people and ministries in our church. We kept asking ourselves what God was thinking. What had we done wrong? Why would he move us when we are so happy serving him, and I was happy as president of a company that was growing and doing well, and relationships with the people in the company were going great. Life was great. **Lesson Learned: Sometimes, God does the unexpected when things are going great to test your faith in him and take you in a different direction and further on your journey.**

A large, privately owned company headquartered in Houston had a division headquartered in Elkhart, Indiana, that needed a new president. This division had two plants in Tennessee, one in Alabama, and one in Indiana. They had gone through three presidents in three years, and they were looking for a leader who could help build morale and set a new direction. It was smaller than the company I was currently leading, but the opportunity seemed very appealing, like it was where God wanted our family. We prayed about it a lot, and I met with the leadership team; I liked them very much. I liked the chairman of the company and his vision for the company. Kay and I made the decision to take the job, as it seemed so right for lots of reasons. God was really giving us the yes signal this time, with no doubts. The company was great, and I learned to love the people and their hearts and willingness to change. They had been through a lot in the years before I came, going through three presidents in three years with me being the fourth. There was no doubt God sent me there to impact their lives and for them to impact me and continue me on my path to becoming a servant leader.

We started this new adventure in October 2003, and it was a great move. The people were great; we joined another great church, Nappanee Missionary Church in Nappanee, Indiana. Kay and I started a newly married class that started with four couples and has grown to about eighteen couples. I was elected to the church board in 2011, and Kay is helping in children's church.

Then, in late 2008, God showed up again with another test. I was asked by the chairman of the company to take an assignment with another of the companies they owned. I had turned it down twice before, because it just didn't seem right. But the third time, I agreed. This company had been struggling since it was purchased, and it needed a new direction, as it, too, had been through several leaders during its history. The economy during that time, as we all remember, was struggling badly and hurting this business like many others in our country. But they said I didn't have to move and could travel to the plants in Fort Smith, Arkansas, and Cincinnati, Ohio, during the week and be home on weekends.

So, from January 2009 until I left the company in April 2010, I traveled almost every week, leaving on Monday mornings and coming home late on Friday nights. This was a different kind of experience for me. I was humbled by several events during the fifteen months I was there. The markets this company was in (transportation) were impacted greatly by the economy. We had to shut down the Fort Smith plant due to poor performance; we sold off one of the product lines to another company and moved the other two product lines to the plant in Cincinnati. With these changes completed, my job was eliminated, and at age sixty-one, with the economy in terrible shape, my new big question was, **"Now what, God?"**

As I look back on this period, I can definitely say it was one of the most challenging and frustrating times of my life. I won't go into all the details, but I wondered so often, sitting in lonely hotel rooms traveling to Fort Smith and Cincinnati, what God was trying to teach me. Then, when I lost my job, it was about what punishment God was handing out and what had I done wrong to deserve this. Those fifteen months and the loss of my job gave me plenty of time to think about my life, my relationship with God, and what path God had in store for me. Well, it wasn't about punishment after all; it was about God building my faith and creating a path for me to do what I had often thought, talked, and prayed about for many years. It was to start my own consulting business. If I had not lost my job, I would have never attempted it. At age sixty-one, I would have felt it was too late to start a business, and having a job with a great paycheck was security.

Now, God was giving me the chance to share my thirty-eight years of business and leadership experiences with business leaders, companies, churches, nonprofit organizations, and anywhere else God might send me. So, in April 2010, I set out on a new path to start my own business. It has been an awesome experience, and the success God has blessed us with has been unbelievable. I couldn't have scripted it any better if I had done it myself. God is good!

The other great thing I wanted to share about my journey and God's awesome blessings in my life are that our whole family is now located in the Elkhart, Indiana, area. My oldest son, Andy, who is now twenty-nine, moved here in 2004, when he graduated from college and took a marketing job with Harman International, who has a division here. He married his high school sweetheart, Jesi, and they now have two sons: Will, four, and Sam, almost two. Then, my youngest son, Patrick, twenty-seven, moved here from Wisconsin in 2010 to help me start my consulting business. So, now a bunch of southerners who started out on a journey together in 1991, when we left North Carolina to move to Wisconsin, have now all ended up in the same area in Indiana. That is a God thing and an awesome blessing (especially having those grandsons nearby). My favorite title now is "Pop Pops."

**Lesson Learned: Sometimes, there is pain in the journey, and it's required to move you to where God wants to take and bless you.** As I look back over the past twenty-five years, when my servant leadership really started, I can see that all those moves to other cities and jobs helped us get back into church, develop our talents and skills for serving others, build a strong marriage, learn how to be better parents and brought us closer to God. Our faith grew substantially, and God showed us he could be trusted in all things. All my promotions and moves up the corporate ladder and into new leadership roles helped me learn it was about people—not me—and the more I served, the more joy and happiness I would find. My wants in life became a lot smaller list, and the things that have become more important to me are God, family, and serving others.

I had found my purpose and passion. My new consulting firm and writing this book are about helping leaders see that developing a servant leader's heart is a high calling and can make a major difference in their relationship with God, their own lives, their family, and the people they are called to lead.

**Lesson Learned: My journey has taught me God is always faithful and can be trusted. Sometimes, you have to go through a storm to find God's purpose for your life and find the awesome rainbows he has prepared for you.** I can truly say that I have found many rainbows during my journey. Does that mean I won't see more storms? I'm sure I will when God needs to get my attention, build my faith, and keep me moving through this great journey called life. I look forward to the journey.

## 2. Cares About People

Caring drives the how and why servant leaders lead and motivate the way they do. Someone may be called a leader, but without truly caring about people, they are not a servant leader. Servant leadership is always about people first, not tasks or results. Caring for people is the key, because people accomplish the tasks and actions that produce the results. If you don't truly care about people and take the time to build relationships that have a positive impact on their lives:

- How can you truly lead your people?
- Why will they follow you?
- How can you really expect to discover and help develop people's potential without having a relationship with them?
- If you don't understand your people's needs, goals, and skills, all you are doing is leading generically.
- This means you put everyone in a box, and you are not harnessing the collective ability of your team.

This doesn't mean you have to be best friends with everyone who reports to you, or hang out together after work or on weekends. But it does mean if you are going to lead someone and understand how they think, what their needs are, what makes them tick, and how you can impact their life, you better know more than their first name and say hello a couple of times a month. **Know their heart!**

Caring leaders thrive on the diversity of their teams. They know how to take that diversity, mold it, and make it work. If you are going to build a team, you start with each individual. You need to understand them as individuals before you can develop your team. What are their skills, experiences, likes, dislikes, and goals for work and life? This does take time, and you won't learn this in one big meeting. This kind of relationship is built moment by moment over time, as you build trust in your relationships with each individual. **Lesson Learned: Build trust and your people will move mountains for you.**

Think about the diversity on a football team. Not everyone can be the quarterback or the star. You need people who can bring different skills and abilities. Servant leaders appreciate these differences in people, where others may complain. A servant leader's ability to see the person and his or her potential helps the servant leader work through the differences in the personalities and the things that might drive other leaders crazy.

Because they embrace diversity, servant leaders are great team builders. They understand the power of the team. They know that the better a team can work together, the closer team members will come to fulfilling their own potential and that of the company. Over time, teams led by servant leaders will usually take on the leader's traits. The team will become more positive, willing to resolve conflict, become better communicators, and set expectations for themselves and the team. They will learn to care and rely on each other as a team. The caring will spread and become infectious. Can you imagine what a company might accomplish if they could truly build a caring group of people with a sense of community?

I will admit the recent economic issues in our country are not making it easy for servant leaders to build teams and relationships. With layoffs, terminations, and reductions in pay and benefits, it is creating new challenges for building trust. But being a servant leader requires making the tough decisions that must be made to reduce costs and protect the future of the company. I will talk more about this under stewardship.

Servant leaders see the potential in their people. They work to bring out that potential in their people, which, in turn, impacts the company in a positive way. They help people maximize their skills by equipping and empowering them to try new things, think for themselves, and innovate. While some success can happen on its own and by luck, most of the time, it is achieved on purpose with a plan, actions, and time spent by the leader to support his or her team members.

If you are not a servant leader or don't really care about people, never try faking that you care about people. They will spot a fake every time.

## COUNTERFEIT SERVANT LEADERS

- They hold meetings with their people, telling them how much they care, but their actions don't match their words
- They provide very little feedback to their people
- They ask for little to no feedback on how they can improve
- They provide very little training
- They have few one-on-one meetings with their people
- Communication with their people is usually done through e-mail or memos
- In meetings, they do almost all the talking, leaving little time for questions
- They show little interest in their team members as individuals
- They focus in on tasks, not people

If you give me forty-five minutes to walk with a leader on a tour of a manufacturing plant, I can tell by the reaction of the people what they think of that leader. Some leaders are good at trying to disguise their poor relationships with their people by smiling and saying hello to everyone, but most don't even try to hide it. They act like they are walking through a forest without seeing the trees. When I was president, I always watched for the people's reaction when the leaders gave me a walk-through of their facility. I could tell by the reaction of the people to the leader's smile or "Hello" what they thought of that leader. Or, if I stopped at a work cell to talk to the people, I watched to see if the leader was showing impatience with my questioning of the people and was trying to hurry me along, so I wouldn't ask too many questions.

Then, if I took the time to talk with the people, they were like kids in a candy store. It always felt like they were starved for attention and for someone in leadership to show he or she cared and valued their opinion.

We as leaders often forget or don't realize the positive impact we can have on people by just giving them our time and showing interest.

I also watch a leader during group or shift meetings to see if they are willing to bring up and discuss tough issues and problems, or how the leader reacts to tough questions from their people. Too often, leaders like to have nice meetings, where nothing of substance is covered or resolved. Then, we wonder why people think we don't care or won't listen to them. Meetings were always a way for me to gauge the atmosphere of the group and the leader's relationship with them. Let me add, if a leader hasn't had training on holding effective and open meetings, then it's the company's fault. A leader can only be held accountable for the expectations and training he or she has had. If leaders are open and responsive to their people, you are moving toward having not only their minds but also their hearts. But don't respond or pay attention to their opinions, and you will get blank stares and a team who is just watching the clock.

## 3. Stewardship

When people hear the word "stewardship," many think of giving money or their tithe to the church. The online definition from Webster's states that "stewardship is the conducting, supervising, or managing of something, especially the careful and responsible management of people and things entrusted to one's care".

For me, I know that everything I have been blessed with—my family, job, talents, skills, abilities, and possessions—are provided to me by God. He has entrusted them to me to be used wisely and to impact the lives of people he puts in my life. So, as a responsible leader, I need to be a good steward and manage them well for the owner: God. Servant leaders realize this same principle. For example, they understand that the people they are responsible for leading are in their care, and they take that responsibility very seriously. They understand that to teach and reach people, to have a true impact on their lives, requires leaders who care. They show they care by devoting time, effort, and interest in their team members' lives.

Servant leaders understand that good stewardship is a win-win for everyone if done correctly. The trouble is that in today's world, many leaders want others to be the good stewards and to serve them. In reading the headlines of newspapers almost every day, it is sad to see that many leaders have lost

45

their understanding of stewardship. They have gone from a, "How can I serve?" to, "How can I be served?" They act as though there is something special that comes with a leadership title that gives them the right to steal, abuse their power, and be entitled to do anything they want. Then we wonder why people in surveys find it hard to trust leaders anymore.

We, as leaders, have a high calling to not only set the bar high for what is right for the organizations we lead but also to live it daily in our own lives. Leaders have a tremendous influence through the rules, policies, expectations, environment, and rhythm we establish and support. Then, the people we lead watch to see if our words match our walk. Do we live out what we claim in our meetings, employee talks, mission statements, and policy books? I have found that in many cases, we leaders have failed. We have allowed crazy compensation and perks to get out of hand for leaders, while laying off and cutting the pay of our workforce. We have allowed behaviors to exist that should be unacceptable and stopped dead in their tracks. But, we get "busy being busy" with managing tasks, and we take our eye off the people, our most important responsibility.

No leader is perfect; we all make mistakes. Sometimes it's an error in judgment or a decision that goes wrong. We can become frustrated with the results of the business or the people with whom we work. We become stressed and lose our temper or patience, all normal occurrences that happen because we are human. But mistakes are different than deliberate actions taken, because we believe we are somehow privileged because of our title or power. The sad part is that leaders do it so often, they start believing it's not wrong anymore. They have fooled themselves into thinking it is okay. Truth becomes whatever they declare it to be.

One last thought. If we can get it right with our people by setting the right examples, treating each other with respect, showing good stewardship in the way we manage the assets of the company, we have a very good chance to succeed as a business. **Lesson Learned: People don't expect perfection, but they do expect caring servant leaders who are real and humble.**

## 4. Communicator

We devote a whole chapter to this subject in chapter seven, because it is that important. While caring is the number-one driver of a servant leader, communication is how they show they care. We not only communicate with our words, deeds, and daily actions but also by not communicating what is right at the right time or in the right way. Servant leaders see communication as the building block for building relationships and developing people. Communication shows people how much we really care or that we don't. Communication can build or destroy people and relationships. Communication is so powerful that it has caused wars and destroyed marriages and countries. Words are powerful, but sometimes, saying nothing is worse.

In most companies, there are leaders with different styles of communication. This means in every company some people are being led by great communicators who get it right, while others are being led by leaders who are not communicating, motivating, or developing people. This can create major problems due to the differences and inconsistency of communication taking place between departments and groups. Then we wonder why visions and strategies never take hold and are confusing to the people.

**Lesson Learned: Servant leaders give and seek feedback.** Their people have a voice and are never afraid to give their opinion or offer suggestions. They have a freedom that others within the company may not have. Servant leaders understand that issues, if allowed to fester and grow, become like weeds that need to be cut off at the root. If not, they will choke off the ability of people to achieve great and rewarding things.

Servant leaders understand that one of the biggest causes of problems in businesses today is leaders are not resolving the issues that everyone knows exist, but no one solves. These are issues everyone knows about and are talked about every month in meetings, in the halls, at lunch, and in doorway meetings. People keep asking, "Why don't they fix that issue?" The problem is really a communication issue, because people won't sit down and resolve the issues and conflict.

The real questions is, "Who is this 'they' everyone is talking about?" Has everyone forgotten that the "they" is us?

In meetings as president, when people would say, "They aren't doing such and such," or, "They are keeping us from hitting our results," my response would be, "Who is they? Bring them to me. How did they sneak into our company? Who are these strangers?" Then, I would begin my talk on we get what we allow to happen as leaders. If there are problems, it is up to leaders to communicate with each other and solve the issues or problems. If we don't like what we have, make a recommendation to change it. Servant leaders communicate their expectations and then constantly teach others how to live out those expectations. We will cover a lot more about communication in chapter seven.

## 5. Humble

When most people describe a leader, the word "humble" isn't usually mentioned. But for a leader to be effective, he or she needs to be humble. Of course, all of us can act and be humbled, especially when we do something wrong or are caught in a very bad situation. We have recently seen the scene played out over and over again on TV with celebrities, politicians, and business leaders who get caught doing something they shouldn't. But I'm talking about being truly humble when you have found success, have achieved a lot in your life, and people admire you. That is when it is hard to remain humble and grounded.

To achieve that kind of humbleness requires a person who has developed their God-given spirit, talents, and ability to put people first and their own success in perspective. One advantage of caring about others is that it doesn't give you time to focus on yourself, your achievements, and wants. **Lesson Learned: Caring about others' needs and helping them find their potential becomes a good barrier for keeping selfishness out of your own life and humbleness alive.** These barriers help servant leaders:

- Feel successful because they are helping others achieve
- When success comes, to be thankful for the opportunity
- Know their weaknesses and what to avoid
- Attract followers, because they are real
- Try to grade their own success based on God's standards, not the world's
- Be strong, and stand up for what is right

## NO FEAR OF DOING THE RIGHT THING

The temptations that can come with successful leadership—such as money, fame, power, and people putting you on a pedestal—will come knocking at your door. Then, we must decide if we open that door or keep it closed.

The big problem is many of us open that door just a crack, thinking we are grounded and can manage success well. I have seen many business leaders during my career fight that battle. Some have lost, and most will struggle with it all their lives.

But overcoming temptation by ourselves is almost impossible. To fight these temptations, we will need to use prayer, read God's word, tuck our children in at night, kiss our spouse often, and focus on what is important. Keep close to the most important relationship you need in your life: God. He can help you fight the battle. It is not a battle that he meant for any of us to fight by ourselves. The more I have tried to make Jesus Lord of my life, the easier it becomes to fight off the pull of success. No, I'm not perfect and have fallen many times in my leadership journey. But through God's grace and mercy, my family, and many mentors, I keep moving forward. You must always remember life and servant leadership is a journey, and if you ever think you have arrived, you are in trouble.

## 6. Positive Attitude

It's when a person in the midst of a storm doesn't get scared or troubled, because he or she knows a rainbow is coming even though it can't yet be seen. I, like many other people, enjoy being around positive people, especially those who have proven over time they can come out of the tough times still smiling and ready to fight the good battle all over again. That attitude is infectious and brings a can do spirit to their teams and followers.

Servant leaders see potential and opportunity, while others see problems and challenges. In today's tough economic times, businesses need leaders with positive attitudes who can help their team focus on the goals and objectives. Most all servant leaders bring positive attitudes to their teams. Servant leaders don't let problems overshadow the possibilities. They bring a confidence that helps people work through the issues to find solutions. Positive attitudes are not gained by always winning or not having any trouble in your life. Positive attitudes are built on a faith gained by going through the everyday battles and coming out on the other side. They have learned things are never going to be as bad as you or others thought.

If you were around in 2000 for Y2K, you know what I'm talking about, when I say things are never as bad as we think they might be. We were all scared to death based on what the news people and so-called experts were telling us. Our world was going to shut down we were told. Electric grids would collapse; water would be in short supply. Machines in factories would shut-down, ATM machines would not give you money; bank accounts would be frozen; on and on, the stories came rapid fire. We all went out and stocked up on food, bottled water sales went through the roof, we got money out of our bank accounts, and businesses spent billions to get ready. We all sat in front of our TV at midnight to watch it all blow up and the world to never be the same. Nothing happened; it was over, and we all went to bed.

Having the right attitude is one of the most important strengths any leader or individual can have in life. There is an old saying: "Life is 10 percent of what happens to us and 90 percent of how we respond to it." Attitude is often more important than skills, education, or resources in determining whether we fail or succeed in life. Can you imagine what our family life, businesses, government, and nation could achieve if we could bring a positive attitude to all the situations we face and the people we meet in our life's journey? What a great world this could be!

## 7. Encourager

Servant leaders love to show people they are an important part of the team and that what they do is important. I can think back during my own career and see the many leaders who encouraged me:

- To try new things
- To not give up when I was on the verge of quitting
- By thanking me for doing a good job
- By teaching me that it is okay to celebrate at work when things go right
- By showing me that when tough times come, they were right there with us
- By taking the time to get to know me as a person
- By taking time to help me learn through teachable moments, instead of criticizing me

## 8. Motivator

Servant leaders have that special ability to bring out the best in people. They know the exact things to say at the right time to get people pumped.

They spend time with their people, finding out how they are doing. Their own work ethic motivates people to give their best. They seem to be able to rise above the tough days and bring a fresh spirit to an organization and its people right when they need it most. They motivate people to work on the right priorities at the right time for the best results. Motivation is the energy that keeps a business and the people moving down the right path. Without motivation, too often people are like boats sitting in dry dock, hanging on but going nowhere. I believe most people who succeed in life had people who motivated them during their life's journey. Not all motivation comes from within. Motivation is the "wind in our sails" when there is no wind to drive us.

### 9. Influencer

Servant leaders have a natural ability to influence people, not by doing anything out of the ordinary, but by caring about those they lead. They have a special talent and the ability to influence people to try new things, to get them to move out of their comfort zone, to help their people discover their potential for greatness, and more important, to reach for it with all they have. While many leaders see people as lazy, servant leaders expect the best out of their people. They don't push; they influence, which produces a big difference in the results over the long term. They lend a helping hand instead of walking away in disgust when things aren't going right. If a leader has no influence with the people they lead, it is going to end badly for the people and the company. People are looking for and need a leader who can energize them. Many leaders and companies fail to accomplish success, because they have failed to master the art of energizing and inspiring those they lead.

### 10. Accountability

I laugh when people ask me, "Aren't servant leaders too easy on their people?" The answer I give is always the same: **Lesson Learned: Servant Leaders believe holding people and a team accountable is one of the strongest tools in their "toolbox."** Accountability helps individuals and teams, as well as a business, reach their potential. But what makes servant leaders different is they help their team meet the results. They don't hold a meeting, pass out the goals, and then go sit in their office, hoping the team makes it happen. The servant leader is constantly coaching, teaching, and checking with the team on where they are in meeting the goals. They use metrics, so the team knows the score and what inning they are in. Servant leaders know that sustainable success is not built on hope but a direction, process, actions, and support by leadership. Caring about people doesn't make you weak; it's what drives you to equip and empower the workforce to achieve success.

It's when you don't care about people that meeting goals becomes harder. Because expectations aren't set, people run in circles, chasing and doing whatever they think might work, while the leader focuses on other things. Real servant leadership is always about the people, while other types of leaders focus more on tasks. So, the real question is what comes first as a priority for a leader: the people or the task? I know in my own career, when I was busy working on tasks and the other things I needed to get done, the team felt abandoned at times. When I spent my time with them, working on the big picture and their individual parts of the plan, things got better and results improved.

It's why so many companies today have embraced Lean Manufacturing and Six-Sigma. These processes and continuous improvement programs start with people, concentrate on people, and stay focused on people and teams. Leaders in the company get involved in how the operation is running, and their attention brings hope to the people that things might change. Communication improves dramatically. Almost everyone stays focused on how to look for and make improvements in their little piece of the world. What the people do every day gets measured to help them see the score and how they are doing. It gives them new targets to shoot for and then provides the tools to help them meet their goals. It creates and promotes a better environment for teamwork, setting and meeting goals, continuous improvement, and team building. Lean and Six Sigma are great tools for servant leaders to use for building teamwork, success, and results.

## FOR ACCOUNTABILITY TO BE A POSITIVE TOOL

- People must know their goals. What are they trying to achieve?
- The goals must be fair and reachable
- There is a plan for how they will reach the goals
- The plan lays out who is doing what and when
- There is a timetable for when they must reach the goals

- Metrics are in place to show their results and the improvements they achieve
- Everyone must know what happens if they achieve their goals and if goals aren't achieved

A servant leader's DNA doesn't make them special; it only gives them the skills and abilities needed to impact people's lives. Like any talent, skill, or ability, it has to be used, developed, and maintained. It has to stay focused on people, and anything that takes their focus off people will hurt the servant leader's influence and results. Guard your talent well from the pull that success brings, and see it as a great gift from God to be used to impact people's lives in a caring and positive way, helping them to reach their full potential and find their own purpose and passion in life.

# CHAPTER FIVE

# RELATIONSHIPS OPEN THE DOOR

Every person God has created is given skills, talents, abilities, personality, and a purpose. The rubber meets the road when we begin our journey in life and start to develop and understand our gifts. Part of our journey includes the influence people will have on our lives. These include our families, people we meet—both good and bad—events, struggles, successes, failures, and the things we can and cannot control in our life. **Lesson Learned: "What happens to you in life is not as important as your reactions during and after the events and then how you allow it to impact you."**

During our journey, we will travel down many paths, discovering things about ourselves, other people, and life. Some paths will be good; others we will have wished we had not traveled. When I look back over my own journey, I can see I learned more from my struggles and mistakes than my successes. None of us likes the trials and challenges that come into our life, especially while going through them. But afterward, sometimes many years later, we can look back and see how they helped shape us and provided us with a better understanding of life and ourselves, and to see things with clearer eyes.

The reason I started this chapter the way I did was to point out that while all of us are different in many ways, we also have much in common.

## MOST OF US AT SOME POINT WILL

- Feel alone, rejected, and unloved
- Have financial issues
- Feel very inadequate
- Wonder what our purpose is
- Have failures

## WE ALSO WANT TO

- Feel appreciated and encouraged
- Be around people we enjoy
- Have meaningful relationships
- Work at a great company
- Earn a decent wage

So, while we are different in many ways, I believe we are more alike than we like to admit. We all have hurts, failures, hopes, dreams, plans, and things we want to accomplish. Almost all of us need to work and earn an income to support our families and ourselves. As you look at my second list, you can see that many of these wants could be achieved if we worked in a great company, where leaders cared about the people and built an environment supported by servant leadership principles. Almost everyone needs to find a job with the goal of earning an income and find a company where we can be part of something that excites, inspires, develops our skills, and brings us together with a great group of people.

But in many companies, something happens to people after those first days and weeks of excitement and great expectations when they started their new job. That excitement declines, and they settle into just punching their time clocks or sitting at their desks, watching the clock and praying it will quickly reach the two most important times of their day: lunch and when they go home. So, what happened?

I believe it's because we as leaders forget business is about people. Just imagine what could happen in our companies if we treated our workforce as well as we treated our customers. What if we treated them with that same, "We will do anything for you," that we have for our customers? Companies will try and move heaven and earth and accomplish great and amazing things for their customers. What would happen in a business if leaders would pursue the building of relationships with their people as hard as they do their customers? Can you imagine what kind of team we could build and develop? It would be mind-boggling. We could develop the kind of workforce we all dream of creating.

Many companies hope it will happen someday but aren't willing or don't know how to change their leadership styles to make it happen. The mission statements on their websites that state, "People are our most important asset," are just empty words, filling up space. It's not that companies are evil or don't want to create the workforce in their vision; it's usually because they don't know how, or they have tried in the past, and because it didn't work, they have given up. Maybe their leaders don't understand how to establish relationships built on caring, encouragement, and motivation or they haven't been taught and trained in the importance of these tools in developing a winning workforce. In many cases, the training that is needed is lacking or nonexistent for the leaders to help them learn new ways of developing their workforce. But if they are to turn their company around or build a workforce that can help them build a competitive advantage, they must build relationships. It cannot happen without them. It's like saying a marriage can be built without building a relationship, communication, or caring.

**Lesson Learned: Servant leaders build relationships because they care about their people. Relationships start the spark for competitive advantage.**

## WHEN PARTNERSHIPS EXIST BETWEEN A COMPANY AND THEIR PEOPLE

- *It creates a team environment* where openness, trust, and respect thrive, and everyone is encouraged and motivated to use their skills and talents and develop their potential.
- *The company builds a strong* competitive advantage by creating an environment where leaders and people work together to improve themselves and their company's results, providing long-term security.

Yes, building relationships takes a lot of energy, time, and effort that many leaders and companies feel they don't have time to give. They believe focusing on other issues and challenges is more important than the people issues. They miss the point that people, the ones who do the work, are the key. It would be like a football coach who worries more about the playbook instead of the players, their conditioning, meal program, training, and practice. While all are important, the concentration needs to be on the players if they are going to build a winning team. I believe it's the lack of relationships between the people and leadership that creates the high turnover, productivity and efficiency issues, and the stagnant or declining performance in most companies.

## WHY IT'S HARD TO KEEP PEOPLE IMPROVEMENT PROGRAMS GOING

- It takes a leadership that understands how to build relationships with people.
- People are complicated, and many leaders don't have the patience or training to deal with this complexity.
- Leaders are very busy and find it hard to give the time necessary to build culture-changing relationships.
- It takes an investment of money for new training programs and processes to bring about dramatic change.
- Leaders and managers think it's easier to buy equipment and chase customers and new markets than try to build a competitive advantage by harnessing the collective potential of their people.
- Many companies don't have enough trained and functioning servant leaders on the team.
- Leaders get caught up in the day to day and don't think about the future. The "fire drills" of the day become the rule instead of the exception and eat up their time and effort.

Servant leaders understand that the first step to building a strong company starts with each individual in the company. Obviously, if I say that to the senior leadership of a company with five thousand people, they will start to get that deer in the headlights look and wonder what planet I'm from and then have me escorted out of the building. Just kidding. But it does sound like an almost impossible task. But if we were to examine the military, and a branch like the army, for example, we can see it is possible. The military has always intrigued me, with its ability to take a group of young recruits and train them to fight for their country.

Let's take a look at their process. They take a group of eighteen- to nineteen-year-olds who, until the day they leave for boot camp, are typical young teenagers. They are playing video games, probably hanging out with their buddies, drinking beer, driving fast cars, dating, going to movies, and watching TV, with very few cares in the world.

Then, they leave home on a bus or airplane and arrive at boot camp. They gave up their carefree life for about $1,300 per month, got their hair cut down to the scalp, have people yelling at them all day, sleep in a room full of strangers, and get up early. No home-cooked meals or sweet Mom, calling to them in the morning to get up, just their drill sergeant, yelling obscenities at them like they are the enemy. Then, they have the privilege of walking hundreds of miles, doing thousands of sit-ups, and having all kinds of other unspeakable things done to them. They teach them to go into combat and shoot and kill the enemy and sacrifice themselves, if necessary, for the mission and our country. I know that sounds cold and cruel, but that is the process.

You would think we as leaders of a business could develop a training and leadership process that could help our companies achieve things we never thought possible. If a company could develop that type of process, it would own its markets and customers. It would achieve things it never thought possible. So, how does a company get started with this process?

**Lesson Learned: It starts by having servant leaders who understand the importance of building relationships and then know how to build relationships based on meeting their people's needs.** As we discussed at the beginning of this chapter, most everyone's needs are in the same categories and pretty basic.

Now, I know some are thinking right now, Bill, you don't know the kind of people we have to hire. They:

- *Don't care*
- *Don't have ambition*
- *Don't come to work*
- *Can't pass a drug test*
- *Quit after a few weeks*
- *Can't get along with people or their supervisor*

Yes, in some cases, you are right: not all people come ready and able to accomplish the kind of work we need. The big question I would ask you to consider: **Is your biggest issue you can't find good people, or is it that your process can't keep good people or develop the people who come through the door?** If you added up the number of people you have hired in the past five years and who left on their own or got fired, how big is that number? I also realize that depending on your type of business, you face different challenges in hiring, developing, and training people. For example, service industries, such as a bank or software company, would face some different challenges than manufacturing companies hiring people to work on the manufacturing floor.

In 1996 while serving as senior vice president of the corporation, we were having major problems at one of our southern facilities. We were having major turnover problems and people issues, along with a young leadership team, and were losing lots of money. I was given the assignment to go down, figure out what was happening, and make changes as necessary. My first meeting was with the leadership team, which consisted of a plant manager and the managers of HR, sales, engineering, accounting, and shift supervisors. As I started asking questions, it was easy to see that part of the problem was, as a team, the leaders were not on the same page. I could tell they had not been talking with each other very often about their problems or, more important, how to solve them. A lot of finger-pointing, blaming each other, and excuses was what I was getting. They explained they couldn't find good people, people didn't care, the plant was in a terrible location, and our customers were too demanding. They didn't really offer any recommendations about what we could do to solve the issues or what they had tried. So, I stopped the meetings and told them to schedule shift meetings with everyone, starting the next day. It got real quiet, and the plant manager asked, "Do you really want to talk to the people tomorrow?" I laughed and said something smart like, "No, I'm making it up. I don't really want to." Then I asked, "Why would I ask if I didn't mean it?" I left the room without saying anything other than I was going to take a walk through the plant by myself. I knew I had made my point, and now they would sit nervously in the conference room, talking about what they were going to do.

My walk was interesting. One thing I learned during my career was how to walk a manufacturing floor and spot one that was out of sync and had no rhythm. This was a facility I was familiar with, so I knew most of the people. I spent the next three hours talking to machine operators, set-up techs, and maintenance people. I asked lots of questions and was getting the answers that I should have gotten from the leaders. **Lesson Learned: People on a manufacturing floor know the issues and problems, but many leaders never ask them for their opinion or pay attention to what they tell them.**

They indicated the big problems started when their business started growing several months ago. Because they couldn't keep up, the plant manager had converted the plant to a twenty-four-hour, seven-day, continuous operation. Before this new work schedule, it had been three shifts per day, five days per week, with some overtime. This change had required the hiring of lots of new people and for current people to rearrange their lives for the new work hours. They said we were having tremendous turnover, no training for new people, and the place got worse instead of better. Surprise, surprise, I guess the plant manager pulled the old, "It's better to ask for forgiveness than permission," action. No one at corporate, including me, knew or had discussed with the plant manager changing to a continuous operation before he did it.

I won't go into all the details, but when I held the shift meetings over the next several days, I learned quickly there had been no training and no time to try and develop any relationships, explain expectations, introduce people, and on and on. The new people felt like they had been thrown into a 'war zone.". One new lady, during a shift meeting, held up her hand and asked, "Do you know how much training I have had?" Of course, I said no, and she said, "The supervisor took me to a machine and said, "this machine cost $1,000,000 so don't screw it up. He stood there three minutes to watch me run a few parts, showed me a few pictures and then left and I haven't talked to him in two days."

I don't need to add much to that story for you to imagine the thoughts that were going through my mind. **Lesson Learned: We get the results we allow to happen.** So, let's review the experience this lady had when she joined our company. She received a couple minutes of training, was scared she would break our expensive machine; she was intimidated and had no relationship with her supervisor. No one was talking with her to make sure she was getting off to a good start. If your first few days are bad or miserable, what can you expect as a new employee? My guess nothing, and we wonder why we have high turnover.

As I have repeated several times in my book, I do not believe people come to work to have a bad day. They don't get up in the morning and say, "I hope I have a bad day, I don't want my leader to talk with me or answer any of my questions, and I hope I am ignored." But this plays out over and over during a day at companies throughout our country. Servant leaders know to turn it around will take real relationship-building between leaders and those they lead. Then, it will take companies to see people as their most important asset, even more important than their customers are to them. If they can truly make that "mental switch," businesses will find—and keep—their people and make the improvements they seek.

## THE RIGHT COMMUNICATION HELPS BUILD RELATIONSHIPS

It opens the door to building relationships. It either builds relationships or tears them down. No true relationship has ever been built without people talking, listening, and truly trying to understand each other. Relationships that need to grow and develop a trust between people cannot survive without good communication. It brings people together. Without a two-way dialogue, relationships that need to flourish and last are almost impossible. The ability to really listen is the strength and most important part of great communication. We will cover communication in more detail in a later chapter seven.

## SEEKING TO UNDERSTAND

Each individual needs to develop and improve their skills, talents, and abilities as they perform their work. This, as you can imagine, takes time and effort on the part of a leader and creates challenges to help your people and the company accomplish those improvements. As a leader, if you have just a few people reporting to you, it's easier than a leader who has lots of people or whole departments, divisions, and companies for which they are responsible. One way companies can help their leaders accomplish this task is to provide testing resources that will give the leader an overview of their people's personality style, motivators, key skills, and abilities. I would highly recommend this for most all companies. I know it can be expensive, but so can hiring the wrong people and the cost of turnover and terminations. If that is not available, the understanding will come more from one-on-one meetings with each person, unplanned conversations, and just spending time together. The more openness a leader can create with his or her people, the more effective those people become in achieving their goals and helping the company achieve its. It also helps the leader become more familiar with why a person may act or react in a certain way. It goes hand in hand with showing you care, not just about their work life, but about the individual as a person. People want and need affirmation and encouragement from their leaders.

## SHARED VISION, GOALS, AND EXPECTATIONS

When people come together as a team working towards the same goals they almost always achieve more than they would as an individual. The servant leader knows if he or she can get people working together toward the same results, using their different skills and abilities to help each other and help them understand the leader's vision and expectations for them individually and as a team, they can accomplish much more. Also, if a servant leader can build a team, the members will have each other's backs. Most people have a need to belong to something. So, servant leaders try to develop the goals and challenges in a way that stretches the team's potential so they learn something new and feel good about what they achieve. When one gets behind, there will be an effort by the team to catch up or meet the deadlines together. They will seek success as a team more so than as individuals. Servant leaders set the standard and model the behavior for their team. They don't just throw out the vision and expectations in some meeting or memo and expect the team to get it done on their own. They lead, coach, facilitate, and work with the team to make it happen. Servant leaders help their people accomplish great things working together.

## CREATING A SAFE ENVIRONMENT

If we took a survey, it would be hard to find anyone who wants to work in an unfriendly and uncaring company. People want to work where they have a voice to ask questions, disagree respectfully, offer suggestions, bring their ideas, and feel they are valued and respected. An important lesson that leading people has taught me, **Lesson Learned: Let people speak their mind, and they will know you appreciate them. Tell them to be**

**quiet or you don't have time to listen, and you will lose them and their value to the organization.**

Servant leaders work hard not to embarrass their people in public or in front of the team. They work to build an environment of fair treatment and recognition for both the individual and the team. They create an environment where you work hard but can also have some fun. If you think about work and our workplace, we spend more time there and with our team members than we do with our family or at home. This means our workplace is a very important part of our social interaction. So, if we can make it a safe place, a place where people can come and feel good about themselves and what they help achieve, we will reduce turnover, improve performance, and have a positive impact on people's lives. This creates an environment that allows people to flourish if they put forth an effort and build something good for themselves and the company. Now, that is a win-win situation.

Servant leaders also create an environment where people can be vulnerable without fear of being taken advantage of and an environment where they can share their real feelings, ideas, and concerns. An environment where people can face their disagreements with honesty and are able to work through tough issues is always best for the company and the people.

## HONEST WITH THE FACTS AND NEWS

Servant leaders develop expectations and goals so their people know where the bar is set and what is expected of them individually and as a team. Nothing is worse than not knowing how you did or are doing in your job. If you think about us as human beings, we like to keep score or have some way of knowing how we are doing. The servant leader also lets his or her team know when it misses the mark and needs to step it up. A servant leader doesn't let it slide; they discuss what they could have done differently and what new things to try. The servant leader works with the team to develop new ways of improving and is always asking for their ideas and suggestions.

When tough times come and layoffs and job eliminations occur, servant leaders talk to their people about what is happenings and why. They don't let them hear about it from someone else, on the bulletin board, or in some e-mail. They talk with them like adults and explain it so they understand.

They might not like the news, but they respect the leader for coming to them with honesty when the news isn't good.

Servant leaders reveal their real side to their people. They will show the real deal with all their strengths, fears, and thoughts. People love having a leader who tells them he or she doesn't have all the answers and needs their help. One of the greatest leaders I ever worked for was so honest in dealing with those of us who reported to him. He would call a meeting and say, "I'm stuck with a major problem, and I need everyone's help." He would lay out the problem allowing us to discuss it and give him our ideas and suggestions. **Lesson Learned: Leaders don't always have the answers and it's ok to ask for help from your team.**

## BUILDING TRUST WITH PEOPLE

Because servant leaders believe in participative leadership, their people learn to trust them, because they recognize they care about them as people and not just about what they can accomplish for them and the company. Servant leaders nurture the team members and help them accomplish their individual and team goals, also. It's a relationship that is eyeball to eyeball. It creates an understanding between the leader and his or her people of who they are. When we can build this kind of relationship, it increases the chance success for the company and the individual can occur. Actions that reinforce trust are things like always keeping your word and never promising anything you cannot make happen. During disagreements, servant leaders always treat people with respect: no yelling, arguing, or name-calling. They try and understand what their people value in life. They work hard to balance the needs of the person and the company. Then, when they cannot do that, they will help their people understand the why behind the no. Servant leaders are also not afraid to confront those who don't live up to the values and standards they have established for the team. This helps build trust, because the team understands what is expected, and there are no surprises or feeling their leader is playing favorites.

## DELEGATION

Delegation is something servant leaders see as a tool that helps them train and develop their people and frees them up to concentrate on big-picture issues and strategies. It's a great teaching tool to help people see they can achieve more than they ever thought possible and discover skills and capabilities they didn't know they had. When you delegate as a leader, you are teaching people you trust them to do a good job. You are saying, "I believe in you." You're building them up when they succeed, and you are helping to teach them when they fail. Delegation also helps servant leaders discover future leaders by giving their people the chance to show what they can accomplish. Too often, leaders will not delegate, because they are afraid their people will fail at the task and make the leader look bad. Or, they are afraid someone will succeed and then they will get the credit. Servant leaders love to delegate and never see it as a threat.

## AVAILABLE FOR THEIR PEOPLE

Giving of their time is an area that separates a servant leader from many other types of leaders. They are always available for their people. One of the most precious things anyone has is time, especially in today's fast-paced world. Every company is trying to do more with less people and accomplish work in less time, putting tremendous pressure on their leaders and people. But the real problem isn't time: it's how we use our time. As leaders, what does our appointment calendar look like? What does it say about our priorities? Are they tasks or people? Servant leaders have learned to select the opportunities and the responsibilities they must work on each day. There is a saying in ministerial organizations that says, "People are doing life together." Servant leaders understand that philosophy, and that is why they are available to their people. They believe in people-centered leadership, which means the greatest opportunities lie in impacting people's lives, and to accomplish that, you must be an involved leader. People need help, they have questions, they have ideas and suggestions, and they get upset and need encouragement. Without the right kind of leader, these kinds of needs go unanswered, and people will pull away. They will feel abandoned, and all you will get from them are their hands or brain. To find a competitive advantage, you need your people's heart, their passion, and them fully engaged. Servant leaders want their people to have a "fire in their belly." And for that to happen, they know they need to be available for their people and "help light the fire."

Servant leaders also know the importance of building relationships with their peers and the leaders they report to for the same reasons they build relationships with their people. They understand "doing life together" in business is about getting to know those you work with every day. Without relationships, no person, business, or family can ever reach its full potential. More often than should happen, the leaders in a company find it hard to get along due to jealousy or worry about who is getting ahead of them in the race for importance. These disconnects between the leadership causes them to miss the achievements they all want as individuals and as a company. It creates stress, hidden agendas, and an atmosphere where people are out for themselves instead of the company. It is an issue that needs to be addressed and worked on by leadership if they want to move the company forward.

## RELATIONSHIPS HELP SERVANT LEADERS TO

- Think about someone other than themselves and their own needs
- Learn how to impact people's lives
- Build bridges of understanding with people
- Move out of their comfort zone
- Improve their communication skills
- Learn from others
- Want people in their lives to support them
- Stay grounded

If leaders are not currently investing their time, effort, and energy into building relationships, their people will suffer, and the company will not achieve the results they want. I have seen it played out over and over again in my career. The companies, departments, and shifts that are suffering and not hitting their goals usually have a relationship problem that exists between the leaders and the people. It might just be a small one, but it will hurt the results. Obviously, there are always exceptions that cannot be helped due to the economy or some unforced event that no one could help. One example of that was 9/11. Hotels and restaurants in New York City all suffered the loss of business for a long time due to this event. There was nothing they did to cause that loss of business and nothing they could have done to stop it. I have also seen businesses that had terrible leadership be successful at least for the short term due to luck or some event that created something good for the company and their leaders. But over the long term, leadership and relationships do matter to sustainable success.

Relationships, the kind that make difference, are more than a leader walking through the plant or office smiling and saying hello. Relationships are built by stopping and asking how people are doing, allowing people to ask you questions or suggest ideas and improvements, and even tell you their son scored two goals in soccer the night before. Building the kind of relationships we have been talking about is not completed overnight. It takes time and effort. As a servant leader, you will experience frustration in trying to build relationships, because some people just won't ever want a relationship with you or anyone on the team—in spite of everything you have tried or know to do.

These types of people will create issues for you and your team building. It might even become so bad that they become a threat to what you are trying to accomplish with your people. In those cases, you go through your procedures with your HR department, keep talking with the person who is creating the issues, and then help the individual make a career move. There comes a point when it's time to stop the insanity and stop giving so much energy and time to someone who will never get it. Instead, spend that time with those who do get it and want to develop their potential and be part of something bigger than themselves. One bad apple can spoil the whole cart. You will never win all your battles or all the people. Some people just can't help themselves and don't want any help from others. But what energizes servant leaders is their knowledge that most people do want help and are looking for leaders who can help them accomplish great things.

# CHAPTER SIX

# RUNNING FROM SELFISHNESS

One thing I believe everyone can agree on is there are no perfect people or leaders. We all have flaws, weaknesses, and a selfishness we will struggle with all of our lives. Some of these areas we have recognized in ourselves and are trying to deal with, while some we have not yet seen as weaknesses. We might even have some areas in our life that are out of control and need to be quickly stopped in their tracks, before they take us down and cause harm.

Servant leaders deal with many of those same issues and weaknesses in their lives. In this chapter, we will look at areas that can come creeping into the lives of servant leaders because of their calling as a leader. These temptations and selfish feelings can corrupt their motives if acted upon. They have the potential to destroy the influence the servant leaders have developed with people and weaken the leaders' caring heart for people, causing them to focus more on their own wants and needs.

As anyone in leadership knows, trying to manage and lead others is a tall task. Then, when you add your own flaws and weakness into the mix with those you lead, it can be overwhelming. In my own experience as a leader, I have felt, at times, like the weight of the world was on my back. You find yourself searching for answers that don't seem to come when you really need them. But the ability to search, recognize, and control our own selfishness is a must if servant leaders want to stay grounded in the principles that have led them down their servant leadership journey. So, guarding against the pull of your own selfishness is a key to staying grounded and continuing to impact the people that you have been called to care for and lead.

One thing I have noticed in most servant leaders I have worked with is their ability to recognize many of their own weaknesses and flaws, and how they have learned to exercise some control over them, so they don't hurt others or themselves. That doesn't mean the struggles or temptations that will come knocking will be any less; it just means they have learned and developed the discipline needed to protect them and not allow these temptations to take root and overpower them.

This self-awareness has been gained though the many battle scars, maturity, and wisdom that comes with age and listening to, watching, and learning from others. Many have found that the strength to handle life and its struggles can only come from the strength and wisdom that God provides though prayer, reading God's word—the Bible—and being part of a church. They learned it cannot be accomplished through their own strength or with some magic formula. It comes only from the creator himself. This relationship with God triggers an alarm system (the Holy Spirit) inside them that warns of impending danger if they keep going down their current path. It holds them accountable for their actions and helps them see the impact that path or decision can have on their life and the life of others. Like all of us, they don't always listen and can find themselves in the wrong spot, but they are usually able to identify it and come back to their servant heart senses faster than most.

Having self-awareness helps servant leaders develop self-control, set goals and priorities, live with less stress, and recognize selfishness as it begins to first appear in their personal life, leadership style, and in working with peers. Servant leaders have good skills and abilities to recognize selfishness in others, but to become an effective servant leader, we need to be able to recognize it in our own lives, so we can stop it and stay real to our team and associates. If we don't, we will start to look like a hypocrite, as we try and help others stay on the right path. **Lesson Learned: It's the biblical perspective that states, we should start with the plank in our own eye before complaining about the speck in someone else's eye."**

# HOW CAN SERVANT LEADERS STAY GROUNDED?

- Take inventory of the things that you have done or said that hurt someone.
- What kinds of people cause you to lose your temper or patience?
- What brings you fear as a servant leader?
- What brings you the most joy as a servant leader?
- When you meet people who cause you to struggle, how did you overcome it?
- When you find yourself in a place that causes you trouble or can bring temptation, ask yourself, why am I here?
- In what areas of your life do you need to improve?
- What actions will you take to make those improvements?
- What upsets you the most?
- What makes you the happiest?
- Do you count your blessings every day?
- Do you have trusted mentors and coaches who can help hold you accountable?
- Remember, God is in control, so give him the steering wheel and hang on.

When you start to fill overwhelmed or sense trouble stop, ask yourself these questions, and they might help to give you some clarity and understanding of the situation.

So, let's review some of the temptations, issues, and challenges that servant leaders face, how they can impact their lives, and how they deal with and overcome them in their lives.

# SIX AREAS SERVANT LEADERS NEED TO GUARD AGAINST

## 1. Self-Centeredness

This means that you are only really interested in yourself. You put yourself, your needs, and wants above those of anyone else. It would be impossible to be or become a true servant leader if you were a self-centered person. How could any person or leader who is supposed to care about people, impact their lives, and help them accomplish great things if they are the center of his or her own universe? The biggest words in your vocabulary would be "me," "myself," and "I." Having a leader who is self-centered would be very demoralizing for everyone around him or her. In my experience, I have never met any leaders who were 100 percent self-centered, thank the good Lord, but I have met some who flirted with that character flaw. Many of us go through this when we are younger, when we are thinking about ourselves and our pleasure, happiness, and wants. But our goal should be to grow out of that enough to start controlling it and start thinking about others.

But leaders who have a tendency to be self-centered and cannot control it can and will destroy relationships with their people and peers. They will take credit for accomplishments and pass the buck when failure comes. People will avoid them like the plague when they see them coming. As the old country song says, "It's hard to be humble, when you are perfect in so many ways." The problem is everyone sees this flaw except for the person who is self-centered.

If you are a servant leader and you ever find yourself thinking about how big a difference you make in the results of your company, or that you're the best and smartest leader in the group, get on your knees and pray hard. Start making a list of all the things God has blessed you with and allowed you to achieve in your life. Hopefully, this will bring you to your senses and bring you back down to earth. If not, get ready for the fall.

## 2. Sense Of Entitlement

In business, it means because of your title, position, or length of service with the company, you feel deserving of something special. This attitude seems to be one that is prevalent not only with leaders in business and politics but people in all stations of life. We see it especially in Hollywood, athletes, TV stars, and people of all ages. During my career, I have run into a few who feel they are entitled to things because of their title, but luckily not many. I also have been blessed to have never had a leader I reported to that had this issue. All my former leaders I respect greatly, because they chose to treat the assets of their companies as good stewards and set a good example for others when it came to money and handling the assets of the company.

Many companies have allowed the sense of entitlement to get out of hand from time to time. Entitlements can be as small as special parking spots in front of the building to a feeling that anything you want should be given to you because you have earned it as a leader. However, servant leaders feel they need to set the example for their people and not do anything that reflects badly on them or the company. This can be hard when you work in a company that provides nice perks for their senior leaders. If it's legal and approved by the company, it is not an issue. Nor should it be judged, even though it may seem out of place. Servant leaders, even if it's legal and approved by the company, need to make their own decisions as to whether it feels appropriate or right.

Servant leaders believe the main entitlement in their company belongs to those they lead, who are entitled to have great leaders who lead with integrity, honesty, and encouragement. Now, that is the kind of entitlement we can all live with and be proud of when we lay our heads on our pillows at night.

## 3. Motives

They drive us to make decisions and actions that impact others and ourselves. Our motivations can and do change because of age or situations that take place in our life. I know in my own life, when I was younger, my motivations were a lot different than when I got married and had children. Motivations can be driven by fear, success, doubt, or need. The drivers for motivations are as many and as varied as there are people. Our motivations can also be driven by good and evil.

Servant leaders, as discussed earlier in this book, are motivated by their true caring and desire to impact positively the lives of people. When they lead people in a business, their motivation goes to work to help their associates find and reach their potential for the good of the individual and the business, creating a win-win relationship for all. To help motivate their team, servant leaders spend lots of time communicating, training, observing, and testing to determine the best motivators for their people. They also understand that different people are motivated by different situations, actions, words, training, learning, and people styles. That's why servant leaders will spend more time than most leaders working with each individual, so they understand that person and his or her needs and motivators.

Many businesses still struggle with leadership development and having leaders in place that can create an environment that provides the right motivators for great performance. As mentioned earlier, I believe it's because we put people in leadership roles that are not ready to become a leader, and many companies do not have adequate training programs for developing the right kind of leaders.

## 4. Seeing Success As Something You Achieved

Several things I didn't learn or realize until later in my leadership career that I know many other leaders struggled with in their early years were:

- People helped me achieve every success I ever accomplished.
- I wasn't as smart as I thought I was.
- Real success can came wrapped differently than I thought it would look.
- Struggles bring more lessons than success.
- Challenges are God's way of testing our faith and putting us on the right path.

If I could have started to learn these lessons during my twenties instead of my thirties, I would have saved myself a lot of trouble, struggles, and worry. But the key for leaders is to learn from your mistakes, and don't repeat them. Most of all, remember that people are always part of any success you may find in life.

## 5. Don't Take It Personally

One of the toughest things for any caring or goal-oriented leader is learning not to take things personally. Those are times when others get hurt by your decisions, your team fails at something, people won't listen, you cannot help those who don't want to be helped, or people blame you for some action or results. It is a natural tendency for leaders of all types to take it personally. But it comes with the territory if you are going to be involved with people, make decisions, and be accountable for the results. So, how does a servant leader learn not to take things so personally?

- Remember you are not perfect. You will make mistakes with people, actions, and decisions.
- You will make the right decisions, but others will see them as unfair.
- Don't get defensive, because that can make a situation worse.
- Always try to see things from someone else's perspective, because it may help you understand the other's actions and words.
- Ask yourself what you would have done differently, if anything.
- Learn to forgive yourself. It may not change the situation, but it will help you.

Like lots of leaders, I have made decisions during my career that impacted people's lives in a negative way. These include things like layoffs, closing a plant, reducing wages, and terminating people who did not live up to the expectations established for them. All were very hard decisions to make, but they were ones that had to be made for the good of the company and the team. Servant leaders who care for people will always feel bad about making these kinds of decisions and actions. If we as leaders ever get to the point where these decisions don't bother us, we need to check ourselves really well and ask for help. As servant leaders, we will be called on to make tough decisions from time to time that will impact people. But in doing so, we need to do it with care and an understanding of what the people will be going through. Always treat them with dignity and respect.

## 6. Letting The Noise Get To You

From time to time, we can all become overwhelmed by work and the hardballs that life can throw at us. Leading people, making tough decisions that impact people's lives and trying to balance everything in our lives can bring us to a point of exhaustion and to our knees. The noise and clutter of life wears us down, and we need to take a break to get away from it all, and let our mind and body catch up with our purpose and rediscover what is really important to us.

## Dealing With The Stress Caused By What I Call The "NOTS" In Our Life

- *NOT* spending enough time with our families
- *NOT* focusing on the important things in our life
- *NOT* accomplishing our goals or those of our team
- *NOT* impacting people's lives
- *NOT* taking care of our health
- *NOT* finding any free time for ourselves
- *NOT* seeing our weaknesses
- *NOT* building a stronger faith relationship with God

## HOW DO SERVANT LEADERS WORK THROUGH THEIR TOUGH TIMES

- Pray, and ask God to give them the wisdom, direction, and faith to trust and follow him.
- Look for the lesson in the season they are going through. What is it telling you about you?
- Understand what brings them joy and what makes them sad.
- They rethink their priorities, and set them in the right order.
- Spend real time with their family.
- Take some time off from work. Go on vacation with their family.
- Keep impacting people's lives in a positive way, and it will restore the joy and energy in their life.
- Don't let others steal their joy.
- Perseverance. Keep on keeping on.

When I was young, my mom had this saying about tough times, "This is just a season you are going through, and it too shall pass." We can all help seasons pass quicker by our attitude and how we respond to those tough times. Remember the old saying, "It doesn't matter how many times you get knocked down that counts; it's how many times you get back up that's important." **Lesson Learned: It's easier to get back up when people are counting on you than when it is all about you.**

# CHAPTER SEVEN

# COMMUNICATION IS THE GLUE

One of the things I have learned during my life's journey is that people are meant to do life together. We accomplish this through relationships with God, our spouse, family, friends, coworkers, and the many other people God will put into our lives. We all have a need to have relationships with others. So, for our relationships to grow in a positive way, we need to learn how to really communicate with one other. I know when you hear me say that we need to communicate your first thought is, I already know how to communicate; I do it daily. But do you really?

I believe that communication is the main building-block for all our healthy relationships in life and the workplace. Communication can bring a company and its people together as a team, or it can separate them and potentially tear them and the business apart. Leaders in any organization set the communication strategy, rhythm, and style within their business and with the people they lead. It's much like a parent, who creates the communication style within the home. The children will learn from their parents and will act out what they see and hear. They will communicate in the style they have seen and been taught.

**Lesson Learned: While most leaders and companies talk about the importance of communication, I believe it is the number-one problem in business today. It is the root of almost every problem in the business.** It keeps companies from resolving the issues and problems they talk about almost every day yet never resolve. It keeps both the business and the people from reaching their potential. It's not that people within a business aren't talking each and every day, but in many cases, it's the wrong kind of communication; it's the kind that doesn't get through to people or make a difference in the results. People are talking at each other but not communicating with each other.

Most of the communication that takes place in a business has more to do with giving out information than using it as way to really make a difference, bring about change and create an organization that helps everyone develop their full potential.

## In This Chapter We Explore

- Communication in the workplace
- What tools servant leaders use to build a partnership between them, their people, and the company
- How an effective communications strategy can help a company and its people form a bond and develop a unity that helps them accomplish more than they ever thought possible

One of my favorite quotes on communication is from William Yates, who said, "Think like a wise man, but communicate in the language of the people." This should be the communication guide for every company in business today. Too often in business, we think we need elaborate and fancy meetings or some grand strategy to communicate with our people and get them excited about working hard and giving us their all. All it really takes are caring servant leaders, who speak the language of the people and provide what people want from their relationships. People want leaders who:

- Listen to them
- Give them feedback
- Resolve conflict
- Encourage and Motivate

## ARE WE USING COMMUNICATION EFFECTIVELY IN BUSINESS?

The communication options that businesses and people have available to them today are almost endless and unbelievable to someone of my generation. When I talk to sales groups about my first years in sales, when there were no cell phones or GPS to help you in your job, I get that "Wow, he sure is old," look.

When we were on the road, every several hours, we had to stop and find a pay phone to call the office to see if we had any messages. We had to stop at gas station after gas station to get directions. I remember when Chicago O'Hare Airport had about as many pay phones as people. But today, I carry my BlackBerry around like it is glued to my hand, and when it makes that little noise alerting me to a call, text, or e-mail, I'm like a kid in a candy store: I can't wait to see who it is. Times sure have changed.

Advances in technology have opened up so many options for communicating that it can keep us connected 24/7 if we desire.

## OPTIONS BUSINESSES HAVE FOR COMMUNICATING

- Voice
- Words
- One-on-one meetings
- Group meetings
- Landline phones
- Cell phone
- Conference calls
- Pagers
- Voice mail
- Mail
- Fax
- Telegram
- Answering machines
- E-mail
- Memo
- Handwritten letter
- Typed letter

- Text messages
- Bulletin boards
- Video conferencing
- Skype
- Twitter
- Facebook
- LinkedIn

I'm sure I left something out, but if we can't find a way to communicate with somebody today using one of these choices, we aren't trying very hard. However, even with all these options, I'm convinced we are seeing less effective and life-impacting communication. **Lesson Learned: Many of these new communication sources have made us lazy in our communication;** we feel when we have passed on an e-mail we have completed our part, and we use the many communication choices at the wrong time or inappropriate times.

An example of the kind of laziness I'm talking about occurred several years ago, when, as president of a company, I watched two of my leadership people, whose offices were right next door to each other, have an e-mail battle for over two hours, trying to resolve an issue. They were having some conflict that was the typical sales and manufacturing battle that happens almost every day in business. After being copied on every e-mail (another bad habit of today's modern communication styles) and starting to feel the blood boiling in my body, I finally got up and marched them into my office to do some teaching and stop the madness. My "little sermon" was on the following:

1. Conflict is resolved face to face.
2. E-mail is informational only, not to be used to settle conflict.
3. Quit trying to copy the world so you can cover yourself or find allies.
4. I expect my senior leadership to talk with each other, not at each other.
5. E-mail doesn't allow you to hear the tone of someone's voice or see a smile or body gesture when discussing a tough issue.
6. Last but not least, quit copying me on every e-mail. If you want my help, come and get me, and let's sit down and talk with each other.

I really do believe e-mail may be the least effective way to lead people, but it seems to be one of the most popular ways leaders communicate with their people today. I have watched way too often, as people try and resolve issues or conflict with those who report to them and their peers using e-mail with little success. Now, before I sound like some saint, I have to admit that I am guilty of having used e-mail for those purposes at times. But too often, it can waste people's time and shows the workforce and all those copied on the e-mail our inability to resolve our conflict.

I also witnessed a sales representative that I was traveling with accept a call on their cell phone while sitting in front of a prospect and in the middle of the sales presentation. Now, as you can imagine, the visit went downhill from there. The ride home for the salesperson didn't go very well, with me preaching about their mistake. I could go on for a long time about the many times I have heard very private cell phone calls in meetings, restaurants, and on airplanes, which should have been made in a very private place, but the person went on like no one could hear. I know all of us have seen and heard what I am talking about. So, now that I have that off my chest, let's discuss communication from a big picture point of view.

The best definition I have seen on communication says that communication is about getting through to people. It's about meaning exchange, not word exchange. It's more than just giving out information. There is lots of information that needs to be shared and talked through with people in business, such as vacation and holiday dates, payroll information, purchase orders, sales and financial reports, monthly statements, facts and figures, CAD drawings, and on and on the list goes. We told ourselves the computer age would usher in a new area, where businesspeople would have more time and less work to do. However, I believe it has created more for us to do, because we have so much information to read and analyze to help us manage our companies better. Or at least we think it does. While it is a blessing, it is also a curse.

But real communication is about leaders getting through to their people to make a difference in their lives, performance, and the results of the company. Servant leaders understand that without good and effective communication, people will have a hard time understanding what is expected of them, and the communication just becomes a bunch of clutter that makes it hard to get through to people in a way that makes a difference and shows we care.

## WHAT SERVANT LEADERS COMMUNICATE TO THEIR PEOPLE

- Their leadership style and their expectations, so their people understand
- The company's strategy and their part in making it happen
- Their individual goals, why they are important, and how each individual will be measured against those goals
- The system for offering suggestions and ideas
- The feedback system and how it works
- How the discipline system works
- The system for getting conflicts resolved
- How to ask for help
- Expectations for teamwork
- They are appreciated and valued as a person and a team.

**Lesson Learned: Good communication starts on the first day a new associate starts work.** I have observed so often that one of the weaknesses in many companies occurs the first few days after a new person starts to work. As I shared in an earlier chapter, they are intimated by the machinery or working with a new group of people they don't know and who don't make them feel very welcome. It's like throwing someone who can't swim into a swimming pool and expecting them to swim without teaching them how to do so correctly. We assume they can catch on, or that the supervisor or team leaders are effective in communicating the process to new associates. What we find is they are good at providing information, but that is different than making a new team member feel welcome or a part of something new and exciting, and sharing expectations, values, and how work gets done. There are companies that have great programs, but there also many companies who don't have the proper system and process in place to assimilate new people into their organization correctly. They leave it up to the supervisor or team leader, hoping they have a process. I believe it is a weak link in the communication process that needs to get fixed. There is no day like the first day to make a good impression on a new hire. As our moms always taught us, first impressions are important.

# A SERVANT LEADER'S LIFE IMPACTING COMMUNCIATION SKILLS

## I. Listening

During my career, I noticed that effective leadership had more to do with listening skills than strategy, barking orders, or telling people what to do. I watched as the leaders who listened to their people the most built a strong bond of trust with their people. Their people worked more efficiently and complained less. Why? Because listening says to people, "You are important to me. I care, and I want to understand your ideas and how I can help you."

Listening is important for a servant leader, because he or she can find out from those in the battle and in the trenches what is going on. These are the people who have to stand in a plant when the temperature is 100 degrees during the summer. They are the ones who feel the pressure from all sides to meet production, get reports out on time, meet customer demands day after day, and usually struggle the most to make ends meet due to the current economic climate.

Listening is important to understanding the real story of what is going on. Appearances don't always tell the real story. I can remember very few occasions when visiting a facility while I was president that it wasn't clean, everything was in place, and everybody was on their best behavior. Why? Because the managers and leaders knew I was coming, and if they could make a great impression, maybe I wouldn't ask as many questions or come back for another couple of months. But they soon learned I would be back every six weeks, and I always talked more to the people in the trenches to find out what needed to be fixed or improved. **Lesson Learned: Asking questions and listening are two of the most effective tools in accomplishing a caring and vibrant workplace**. It wasn't about catching people doing something wrong. I always felt if we knew what the problems were and could be honest with each other, we could work together to solve those issues and problems. A servant leader doesn't want his or her people hiding problems. That is why they work so hard to create trust and a, "Don't kill the messenger" environment.

On many occasions, the information people provided me was a different perspective than that of the plant leaders and managers. Sometimes, leaders see things from a thirty thousand-foot view, while those closest to the action see it firsthand. They have to live and work in it every day. That doesn't mean they are always right or have a clear understanding, but if we don't listen to them, we lose the opportunity to understand them better and see their point of view, no matter what it might be. It also gives us as servant leaders the opportunity to answer their concerns and for them to see we really do care—even if we can't change every situation they think is wrong or bad. At least they know our thinking and why we can't or won't change something.

Servant leaders see one-on-one conversations with people as a great opportunity. It's a time when a servant leader sits with an associate or stops by his or her workspace and talks about that person's needs, desires, and hopes for life; it's time for the associate to discuss goals, family, and ideas on how to make the job, department, and the company a better place to work. It happens often, not just once in a while. It's the servant leader's way of showing he or she really does care. Anyone can say they care in words, but showing it by our actions is what cuts through the sweat, hard work, and frustrations of the day. One great way to accomplish this is at lunch. Everybody has to eat lunch so make it a point to have one-on-one meetings with people at lunch. You don't have to go out; you can bring a sandwich and learn a lot about someone during that time.

The more responsibility and the more people a servant leader has reporting to him or her, the more important listening skills become to the leader and his or her team. It is needed, so the servant leader can keep building that bridge with his or her people. Too often, when we get really busy as a leader, we forget about our people, and time can pass quickly before we realize it has been a while since we spent time with them. Time is the most precious thing we have so when we share it with someone it says they are important to us. **Lesson Learned: Listening helps servant leaders see the differences in their people**. Who needs the most help, who catches the vision, and who doesn't? It allows us to see that people learn in different ways, and all have strengths and weaknesses that need to be worked with and addressed. The one important issue that you don't hear many leaders address or talk about is that men and woman are different, which does require some adjustment when working with them. Men and women process life differently; we are each driven by many different desires and needs. Men can compartmentalize issues and challenges, while women combine many things to process issues and challenges. Women, by nature, are better listeners, while men want to jump in and fix things too quickly, when better listening is what is needed. I can say without doubt and with conviction that when I took my plant tours, the ladies spoke more openly and were willing to talk about issues more than the men. Servant leaders listen differently, depending on the person and the gender. Don't kill me; I'm just stating what I have learned through my own experiences.

## THE BARRIERS TO LEADERS LISTENING

- *Running out of time* to do their jobs in today's fast-paced business environment is creating lots of pressure on leaders. Today, many leaders are wearing two hats—as a manager and a leader—reducing the precious time they have to lead and impact people's lives.
- *Distance between them and their people.* Many leaders have people scattered at many locations and, in some cases, all over the world. They will use many of the communication tools we talked about earlier, which means they have to work harder at building relationships with their people.
- *They are inexperienced at leading people* which means they will need lots of training, coaching, mentoring, time, and experience.
- *They feel the pressure of leading people* and avoid listening or meeting with their people.
- *Distractions* in their own life or at work keep them from listening to make a difference.
- *They sometimes find it hard to listen* to people they don't like or are difficult to lead.
- *They find themselves feeling the pain* of their people when they listen, so they start staying away.
- *Things aren't going well with the company or their department,* and they don't want to be asked tough questions.

There are many more, but these are the barriers leaders will face the most. When leaders start the process of listening and communicating, they do not want to stop, because if they do, their people will notice very quickly and wonder what is happening. Leaders also need to ensure that when things are not going well with the company or the results it is achieving, they need to come around more. Servant leaders don't run or hide when things get tough; they get closer to their people and communicate more.

## 2. Giving Feedback

Servant leaders believe if people aren't told what they need to improve in their performance, attitude, behavior, and action they won't know how or what they need to improve. As the old saying goes, "You can't improve what you don't know about." Many companies have at least a once-a-year performance review for their people, but they are usually very generic and reviewed by the supervisors, managers, or leaders. As the role and responsibility of a person increases, the review requires more time and more give-and-take during the review. It's something that most companies need to put more emphasis on and see it as an important tool for helping their people and the company reach their potential.

I have to admit that I didn't always do my reviews with the people who reported to me as well as I should have, especially during my early leadership days. It's the "busy, being, busy syndrome" that usually causes the problem. Most HR departments have a very good system, and they send out the paperwork for the reviews on time, but the leaders and managers keep them on their desk too long and are almost always late in holding performance or annual reviews with their people.

Shame on all of us for being late and not giving this important process the attention it and the people who report to us deserve. This is a very important tool in a servant leader's toolbox. It allows the servant leader to have a real conversation with his or her people on their performance, what needs to be improved, and to give people the chance to talk one on one with their leader to discuss concerns, issues, and goals. It should be a real give-and-take discussion on how they are doing, what needs to be improved, and the action plan to help them improve.

Holding performance reviews is another area where leaders need training. I have sat in on many reviews during my career and could see how nervous the manager or leaders were during the meeting, how they sugarcoated some of the information, didn't cover some tough issues that should have been covered, and tried to hurry the review so the person they were reviewing didn't have time to ask too many questions. This is a time for real soul searching and building a relationship with your people and not just satisfying the HR department. It's one of a leader's most important responsibilities.

This is a time that real trust can be built between the leader and his or her people. There are several ways the leader can help the meeting be successful and something to which people look forward:

- The meeting needs to take place in a comfortable setting that is relaxed, private, and quiet. I once saw a supervisor hold a review with an employee out by their noisy machine, with people running all around. That screamed, "I don't care about you, and this is just something I have to do."
- Set aside enough time so a real conversation can be held. If the meeting needs more time due to the issues that are raised, or the meeting needs follow-up, reschedule so it can be completed without any important issues left hanging.
- Start by asking questions about the family and other things you should know about them, since you have been having some one-on-one conversations during the year. Relationships are built over time, not with a one-time event.
- There should never be any real surprises during their performance review if you have been talking with them during the year.
- Be ready to take notes, but don't be like a stenographer taking notes in a courtroom. Taking too many notes will make them feel uncomfortable.
- Start with their strengths and things they do well: the positives. Give them a chance to add some topics they think you might have missed or you didn't know about.
- Go over the issues or goals they need to improve on before the next review. Again, give them a chance to voice their thoughts and comments.
- Discuss any goals or objectives they were previously assigned and how they did. Hopefully, if they were assigned, they are measurable; if not, it becomes subjective.
- Discuss issues from the last performance review and the current status of those issues or activities.
- Set some goals or improvement areas that will be discussed at the next review.

- Ask them to give you feedback on things they feel you can do better as their leader. This is never a time to be defensive. It's a time to listen and, if needed, ask for clarification and examples.
- Let them have the chance to make any last comments or ask questions.

These sessions give the servant leader and his or her people a chance to be really honest, speak truth, and build a relationship that can stand the test of time and events. It also helps your people feel appreciated; they have a voice and can sit down with a leader who cares not just about their performance but also about them as a person. I believe that these formal reviews should be held once a quarter, where there are issues that need to be resolved, need some extra coaching, some important improvements have been identified, and where ongoing, follow-up needs to take place. Then, there are the important hallway meetings and informal conversations that often take place in the office or out on the manufacturing floor. They are very important to developing the open communication every business needs.

## 3. Resolving Conflict

**Lesson Learned: Life does not happen without some conflict.** Conflict is created because we are all different and come to work with our ideas, perspectives, expectations, backgrounds, wants, and needs. Actually, conflict starts early in life. You can see it played out when you put a group of two-year-olds together with some toys and watch them push a little and try and take toys away from each other. But what is interesting to watch is how they work out their conflict. A few minutes after the crying, pushing and tugging over the same toy, they are playing and laughing with each other like nothing ever happened. If we adults could just learn to work and play like those two-year-olds, we would all be happier, resolve our conflict a lot quicker, and learn to forget it and move on.

When I first started out in my career, the word "conflict" would give me a stomachache. The word itself brought about negative thoughts for me. I avoided it at all costs and usually kept my mouth shut in meetings where tough subjects were taking place. I would let people win an argument, even if I knew I was right. But luckily, with some good mentors and coaches and a growing understanding that conflict in business is necessary, I learned that it was through this process that businesses move forward. It is a normal process that allows leaders to talk through all the options, give everyone a chance to give their opinion, and come together as a team, agreeing to the right decision or path they should take and then supporting it as a team and working to make it a success.

## AREAS THAT CAN CAUSE CONFLICT IN BUSINESS

There are many issues and day-to-day events that can and do cause conflict between individuals and groups. Some are easy to forget, while others take some time to resolve. Then, there are those times that issues and conflict cannot be resolved and tough measures and decisions are called for. We address the more normal types of conflict in business first. These conflict areas are:

- Strategy discussions
- Feelings of being mistreated or ignored
- Compensation
- Customers
- Company policies
- Problems between departments and their leaders
- Resistance to change
- Lack of communication
- Escalation of small issues into big issues
- During periods of layoffs and plant closings
- Differences in leadership styles within the company
- Difficult people

The first step in resolving conflicts is for leaders to recognize it and take action to resolve it. In my career, I have seen simple issues turn into bigger ones, because the leader or leaders avoided the situation and let it continue, or hoped it would go away. **Lesson Learned: Leaders need to realize that what they are really paid to do is to solve problems and resolve conflict.** Every day, leaders are involved in hundreds of decisions that need to be made. Many times, their decisions will be made after receiving lots of information from different sources, which can contain conflicting information and recommendations. Then, they must resolve all these differences in opinion and information and make a decision. Also, almost any decision a leader will make will impact people. That is why leadership is not for the faint of heart.

So, how does conflict get revolved? This is the million dollar question and one of the biggest struggles and areas many leaders have never been trained in or feel comfortable handling. So, let's look at what servant leaders think about conflict resolution.

## FOR CONFLICT TO BE RESOLVED SERVANT LEADERS BELIEVE

- *People need to check their egos* at the door. As all of us know, many leaders have at least some ego. It's both their strength and weakness. But servant leaders have learned to check theirs.
- *Every person can have a little piece of right* in any argument. No one person has all the intelligence in the room. Different perspectives are needed when working through tough and important issues.
- *Don't make it personal.* It's not about who is right or wrong but what is best for the company and the people. When you try to embarrass someone or make them look stupid, conflict can go in the wrong direction or spiral out of control.
- *Patience is required* if conflict is going to be resolved. Big decisions take time and effort. Sometimes, calling a time-out is needed to calm everyone and clear the minds. Then, all can get back together to work though the conflict.
- *Being humble,* which means I don't have all the answers, and I'm willing to listen to other ideas and suggestions.
- *Letting someone present their ideas and perspective doesn't* mean you agree with it; it just means you respect them as a person and are willing to listen. Realize that we may see the same reality differently.
- *Use positive words.* If we use too many negative words, it can take the discussion in a wrong direction.
- *Control your emotions.* You will get frustrated during conflict, but what is important is what you do with those emotions and feelings. Don't let them control you.
- *Seven percent of communication* is in the message, and the rest is in the tone of voice, nonverbal expressions, and gestures. So be careful.

- *People need to make a commitment* that once the conflict is over, it's over. Let's at least act as nice as two-years-olds, who forget and go back to playing with each other nicely.

As stated earlier, conflict is a normal occurrence in business. But for it to become a positive and used as a tool to make the right decisions, it must be resolved and not left to fester, as we would say in the South. Conflict can lead to better communication in a business, or it can block it. If companies see conflict as another form of communication and not a nuisance, and a way to bring issues to the forefront, it can become a big positive and will show their people they do care and will listen to their issues and problems. But if companies see conflict as a terrible thing and something to be avoided, or they try to manipulate it or shut it down, they will miss the opportunity to solve the many problems that are holding them back from developing a sustainable competitive advantage for their future.

## 4. Encouragement

Do you know anyone who doesn't like to be encouraged? Who doesn't like to be told they are appreciated, doing a good job, or are important? All of us can think back over our lives and remember coaches, teachers, family, and leaders who encouraged us to try and accomplish new things. They told us when we failed, we won't be remembered for the failures but for how many times we got back up and tried.

**Lesson Learned: People want to know that the people they are doing life with really care about them**. Anybody can be nice and give encouragement when things are going well. Real, life-changing encouragement makes a difference when we are struggling or we have gotten down on ourselves, and our leader or a special person picks us back up. They give us hope and encouragement to keep on that path, or they help us see we are on the wrong path and help us get moving again. People who feel encouraged in their workplace are:

- Treated fairly
- Receiving feedback
- Given many chances to express their feeling and ideas
- Trained in the expectations for their job
- Trusted
- Recognized

- Dealt with honestly
- Innovative
- Ready to climb mountains for their leaders and team
- Have a leader who cares about them as a person

Because of their encouraging style, servant leaders will usually develop teams that will work hard to follow their leader and meet expectations. They might not always jump on the bandwagon at first, but they will come around and give it all they got. They might not always succeed when they try, but try they will.

Giving encouragement is one of those soft skills that businesses talk about from time to time but not often enough. They certainly don't spend enough time training supervisors, middle managers, and leaders about this skill, the purpose and the impact it can have on people, and what encouragement looks like in the day-to-day activities of leading people.

With this said, leaders must understand that if the encouragement is not real, people can pick it out from a mile away. In my career, I have been around people who try to motivate or encourage, but you can tell their motivations and interests were all wrong. That is why servant leaders are so good at it: they are real. It is driven by their purpose, which is caring for people and their desire to help people reach their full potential in life. **Lesson Learned: Servant leaders see the whole person, not just the person who comes and does some work. Servant leaders are in the business of growing people.**

Most people in a workplace are hungry for someone who can encourage them to try new things and to show them they are capable of achieving so much more. Servant leaders bring that special something that helps people feel energized toward continuous improvement not only in their work but also in their life. They move people to do what is important not only for the company but also to try things that can have a positive impact on them as a person and their life. It creates an environment that drives people to discover their capabilities and try things they never thought possible. Then, when other people within the workforce see this happen, it becomes contagious, and they start stepping out to try new things.

Part of the art of encouragement by a good servant leader is looking for small victories to celebrate with his or her people and team. It reminds me of watching my grandson learning to walk. He kept trying to walk and kept falling down. We kept clapping and cheering him on, but on those first several days, he never made more than a few steps without falling down. It didn't make us sad or stop the excitement and celebration of the moment. We didn't say it was terrible he didn't make it, or that he was a failure for falling and not walking yet. What we celebrated was his effort, his attempt to try something new. Can you imagine if we could encourage and celebrate effort like that at work when people tried new things, even if it didn't work? I believe it would not only change lives, but the innovation and effort in attempting new things would help us soar like eagles. Servant leaders understand that developing people and bringing about change is all about incremental progress. Just like my grandson, taking small steps and getting ready to take those big steps when the timing is just right.

Encouragement is also about getting people to think and dream about what could be for them and the company. Servant leaders help them see the potential by shining a light on the possibilities. Think of it this way. You are lost in the woods, it is dark, and you are lost and don't know which way to go. Then, you see someone coming with a flashlight. You are not sure whether to be afraid or excited, because you don't know who it is. The person comes running up and points the flashlight at you. Would you feel safer if the person shined the light in your eyes, so you couldn't see who it was and didn't know what was happening, or if the individual shined the light at your feet, so you could see the path that leads you out of the woods? **Lesson Learned: Servant leaders shine the light on people's strengths and possibilities and then provide the encouragement and help needed for them to travel the right path.**

As we close out this chapter, just a few more thoughts on communication. Servant leaders understand that communication is the glue that not only brings it all together but keeps it together, if done correctly. Nothing gets done without people communicating with each other. But all of us need and want communication that inspires and motivates us. We also want an open and honest communication that creates a safe haven for us in our relationships with each other. **Lesson Learned: Communication is where people, relationships, dreams, potential, and listening meet.** The right kind of communication can take us on new journeys, mend relationships, create a caring and enthusiastic workplace, or it can bring defeat, unresolved conflict, and unrealized dreams. I know which path I choose: the right kind.

# CHAPTER EIGHT

# DIFFICULT PEOPLE AND SITUATIONS

Every business and organization has people who are difficult to deal with. It's part of life and business. Just remember the old saying: "What doesn't kill you makes you stronger." I am a better leader today because of the many tough situations I went through, leading all types of people, even those who were hard to lead or didn't want to be led. No matter how good a leader or how great the company, there will always be difficult people and situations to deal with and handle. There are also varying degrees of difficulty, but for this chapter, I'm talking about individuals and situations that can turn into real stumbling blocks during a servant leader's attempt to build a positive working environment, help his or her people reach their potential, build a team environment, and help the business meet its goals.

## WHAT DO DIFFICULT PEOPLE IN BUSINESS ACT LIKE

- Believe they have all the answers
- Won't listen to reason
- Don't get along with people or a particular person on the team
- Don't follow instructions
- Create conflict for the wrong reasons
- Need training
- Lack discipline in their work

- Don't like their leader
- Hate their job or the company
- Mental or personality issues

What is important for the servant leader is to try and assess the situation as quickly as possible to determine what is going on with this person, what's behind his or her actions and attitude, and how big the problem is, so the leader knows what he or she is dealing with and to help determine what course of action to take.

## THE SERVANT LEADER NEEDS TO DETERMINE

- Is this behavior new for that person?
- If not new, how long has it been going on?
- Is this person new to the organization or team, or is he or she someone who has worked there for a while and is a known entity?
- Is it something that can cause harm to others or themselves? (This is the most dangerous and requires immediate action.)
- Has the leader noticed this behavior, or is he or she being told about it and by how many people? What is the impact of the behavior on the people and the organization?

Servant leaders won't waste much time before taking charge of this kind of situation. They know from experience this kind of situation can have a negative impact on what they are trying to create with their people, team, or department. I have witnessed leaders make excuses for difficult people and then watch as the situation destroys the morale and the team building that has taken place. It also eats up way too much of the leader's and HR department's time. I have done this myself several times, when I thought I could turn around someone who had been with the company a long time and was now creating major issues and problems. I couldn't turn around the individual and finally had to terminate the person.

## ONE DIFFICULT PERSON CAN

- Cause conflict in a department or the company
- Interfere with other people getting their work done
- Change team dynamics
- Hurt the results of the company

- Take up too much of the leader's time in dealing with the situation
- Create doubt within the team about the leader's ability to handle tough situations
- Make people think you are playing favorites with that person

To handle tough people issues servant leaders will usually meet in private, with only the person causing the issues, but the HR department should be aware of the meeting and the situation. However, if there is some reason to fear this person or it has to do with sexual harassment or some very complicated issue, you should have the HR manager or someone from HR in the meeting with you. If this person is of the opposite sex, I would usually have someone from HR in the room with me, especially when I was president.

This meeting is not about confrontation but one of seeking to understand what is going on with that person. In the past, as president or vice president, I have usually chosen to go to a public place (if the person is a direct report) for lunch to create a relaxed atmosphere and make it seem less confrontational. Obviously, if it is some big offense or issue, I would not take them to a restaurant. I'm talking about a behavior that has just started happening, and I'm trying to have a conversation to understand the why behind the individual's behavior. That is just my choice, and a meeting in an office behind closed doors would work just as well if that is your preference.

I start out asking questions about how things are going with the person, his or her work, and if he or she has any suggestions on things we could be doing better. Then, I explain that I wanted to talk about some concerns I had about recent behavior and explain what had been noticed. I would not mention the name of anyone who might have reported the situation to me. The purpose at this point is to create an atmosphere for a conversation between two people. Then, I stop and let the person respond to my questions, and I answer any of his or her questions. It then usually goes into one of four directions:

- The person denies there are any problems and does not know what I'm talking about.
- It is other people's fault and not his or hers.

- He or she wants to know who is telling me about the problem.
- The individual will explain what is going on and understands the problems he or she is causing and commits to improving.

Based on the person's response, you will know which direction to take the conversation. This is not the time to get into any arguments and definitely not to humiliate the person. It is truly a time to gather facts, control emotions, and seek to understand his or her side of the story. No decisions are made at this time, and you indicate to the individual you will get back with him or her after you have had time to think through everything that was discussed. Ask the person if he or she has any last comments or thoughts.

## Develop Next Steps and Direction

I will take my thoughts and notes and meet with the HR manager to discuss my ideas and next steps, ask for his or her opinion, and ensure I am heading in the right direction. These kinds of issues can sometimes end up very badly, and even in court, if there is a dismissal from the person's job. So, you want to make sure HR is aware of what is happening, and you have their input and recommendation.

I would then schedule another meeting with the person to go over my expectations for the changes I want to see in behavior and attitude, with goals established. This will be in writing and a copy given to the person and one placed in his or her HR file. The meeting would again be private, usually in my office. I would ask the individual at the beginning of the meeting if he or she had time to think through our last meeting and if he or she has anything further to comment on or discuss. Depending on their initial attitude, this may be a time to encourage the individual and state we want him or her to be part of our team. Obviously, if the person starts out very negative and blaming everyone else, I would take a very different direction.

I will walk them through the next steps, their goals, and help him or her understand I am there to help. I'll also explain how we move forward. I tell him or her I'm willing to help all I can, but the person needs to follow the plan—without exception. I look for acceptance and commitment, and if he or she agrees, I ask the individual to sign the plan we just discussed.

We then set up a meeting in thirty days to review progress and the expectations we established. During those thirty days, I would be checking with the person and a few others to see if positive changes in attitude and actions are taking place. I'm not looking for perfection, but I'm watching to see if he or she is serious about changing and being part of the team. If the situation doesn't change, I would determine what is causing the shortfall to the agreement we made. If the person is not trying and the same situations are occurring, termination would be the normal selection. Even in termination, the servant leader always tries to show concern for the person and treats him or her with respect.

## DECISIONS THAT CAN CREATE DIFFICULT SITUATIONS

### Change

Change is something lots of people struggle with in any company. When people have been doing something a certain way for a long time, they may find it hard to accept change. When companies have to ask their people to make major changes in how the business is operated or to re-engineer their companies and jobs, people become nervous and are very concerned about how it will impact them, their jobs, and their future. Servant leaders will spend lots of time communicating with their people on why the changes need to be made and how they will impact them. They never sugarcoat or hide the truth. Communication is always in person and with the team or the group that is being impacted by the changes. There is always a lot of time provided to answer their questions and concerns. Too often, leaders announce some new changes in a big meeting and feel they have done their job in communicating what needs to be said. **Lesson Learned: More communication—not less—is needed with changes that impact people.**

### Layoffs and Terminations

Laying off people is always tough, no matter who the person is or their position with the company. Why? Because it impacts people's lives. Especially during tough economic times, many of the people who get laid off had nothing to do with the reason for their layoff. Even though they accomplished what they were asked to do, they still got caught in circumstances beyond their control. Again, the only thing you can do is treat the people with respect and do all you can to help them get through the paperwork and issues they will be facing. As a leader, eliminating people or closing down a facility was always the toughest decision for me. I always felt like I had failed them. Tough decisions are never easy but must be made as a good steward over what has been entrusted to you. Again, the more communication you have with your people the better during these types of situations. We also need to remember the people who are left at your company after a layoff are always watching to see how leaders treat the people who were laid off or terminated. Lead with respect, dignity, and encouragement during these situations.

## Taking Disciplinary Action

Taking disciplinary action against someone can create some tough situations, especially if they remain a part of the team. I always watch how well most sports teams seem to handle this type of situation. They know how to discipline and then bring the team member back in as a part of the team. Then, if they stumble again and don't follow the rules and expectations, they are usually gone. I have disciplined several people during my career for saying or doing some pretty stupid things. It usually had something to do with sexual harassment, or someone cussed out someone, or someone was looking at some inappropriate website. It is usually a fine line between termination and a disciplinary action. Obviously, these types of issues need to be spelled out very well in the policy manual and employee handbook. Again, HR needs to be involved in all these types of situations.

When this type of issue occurs, it usually involves several meetings with the individual, and I always made it a point to meet with the person who felt wronged by that individual. I ask that person, "If you were in my position, how would you discipline this individual?" It gives that person a chance to talk through what happened and how it impacted them. In almost every situation, the harmed person told me he or she wanted that person just to be disciplined and not terminated. I believe what really worked was the person saw my real concern for what he or she went through and how the person felt. I did not brush it under a rug and tell the individual he or she was just being silly or should just forget it. I did care for them and wanted them to be part of the process for how it gets settled. Obviously, if the issue was a major one and warranted termination, I did not give the harmed party the opportunity to choose, as the policy would spell out the disciplinary action to be taken.

Handling difficult people and the situations they cause is what leaders do. It's important that it's always done in the right way. Learning how to do it correctly is developed over time. The first time I ever had to fire someone, I thought I would crawl under my desk. It was horrifying for me. I think in all honesty, I was more worried about me than the individual. If these types of situations are to be handled correctly, someone needs to train the leaders on how to correctly do it. Servant leaders go into these situations thinking about how they would want to be treated if it was them. Also, because of their heart for people, it is natural for them to care for all people and show they care through their actions, even during tough times and situations.

In handling difficult people and situations, servant leaders will lead with grace and respect when working with the person who is causing the difficult situation. But in the end, the decision has to be made based on what is best for the company and the remaining team members. Servant leaders don't run from tough situations or people; they face them head-on to reach the best possible decision for all involved.

# CHAPTER NINE

# STRATEGY: THE "DAILY DOSE"

Servant leaders know that strategic thinking and planning is one of the most important efforts a company should undertake no matter their size. It starts with senior leadership taking a timeout from their busy day-to-day schedules to take an honest look at the business and themselves. A current state review is a snapshot of what is happening in all areas of the business today and then creating a vision and future state for the direction of the business in the future. Strategic planning, in simple terms, is really all about deciding what you want to get done and then doing it.

## AREAS TO REVIEW DURING STRATEGIC PLANNING

- Leadership (vision, mission, and values)
- People (skills, capabilities, and needs)
- Product and service offerings
- Markets, customers, and competitors
- External environment
- Sales channels and territories
- Revenue growth
- Technology
- Infrastructure needs
- Investment
- Goals, objectives, critical issues, action plans, implementation, and execution

- Metrics developed with targets
- Communication of plan to all associates.

As everyone who has gone through strategic planning knows, there are lots of moving parts to each one of these areas, and to move them from words on a page to the results you want to achieve is where the rubber really meets the road. It is where most companies come up short.

## A SERVANT LEADER'S MUST-HAVES FOR STRATEGIC PLANNING

- All senior leadership must be fully engaged in the strategy process and provide real, honest input. It cannot just be the president's vision or ideas.
- Set aside a realistic amount of time to consider the size of the business, what is happening in the business and the challenges the business faces. This is not something you rush, because it is about the business's future and success.
- Use a facilitator from outside your company with more than twenty years of business and leadership experience to lead you and your team through the strategic planning process. The person should have an unbiased opinion, be very honest with you, and keep the process moving.
- You will need to consider both internal and external issues and events.
- Work hard to develop a distinctive strategy that does not mirror your competitors'.
- The first big step in the process is more about strategic thinking instead of looking at the numbers, which many companies tend to do. I believe many companies spend more time on the numbers, because their leaders are not comfortable dealing with the real issues and making tough decisions. Numbers are old news.
- Strategic thinking should help you jump-start the process and get the leaders dreaming and talking about the "what ifs and possibilities." People must feel free to speak their minds if this is going to work. Servant leaders want a dialogue with real honesty and participation.

- Goals, action plans, and implementation schedules—with timelines showing who is responsible—must be developed and followed.
- The goals that have been established must be measurable, fair, and tracked. Monthly and quarterly meetings must be held to review what is happening and to hold everyone accountable for what has been agreed to by the group.
- Strategic planning is not an event and must be revisited often to make adjustments as needed and check assumptions to see if they still hold true.
- One of the most important parts of the whole strategic planning process for servant leaders is the communication plan so all associates understand the strategy and the expectations for their behavior and actions to support the strategy and the accountability.

Servant leaders know the lack of communication is the big disconnect for why most strategies never make it out of the executive suite and down to the people who have to make it work. The big question I would ask our senior leadership after we would finish our strategic planning was, "Who is going to talk to the third-shift supervisor, and how will they know what their responsibility is, so they can develop their department's daily dose?" That was my test question. I would usually get strange looks and that strategy is for "big boys," not third-shift supervisors, look. We forget somebody has to communicate, implement, and follow-up on the strategy for it to be successful.

## WHAT IS THE "DAILY DOSE"

It is the blocking and tackling that takes place in business every day: those important actions that must happen and on the right timeline if the strategy is going to have a chance of being successful. If you go back and look at the list at the beginning of this chapter, you saw a list of the areas that must be covered during strategic planning. Each one of these areas will contain strategies, objectives, goals, and action plans that will then be broken down and assimilated to the leaders and departments responsible for making it happen. Servant leaders will then break it down further, similar to a football coach who develops plays with specific actions for each player as part of an overall game plan.

This creates the daily dose for who will do what, when, and the results required. It's basically taking a big-picture strategy and breaking it down to manageable objectives, goals, actions, and the desired results. As the old saying goes, "You don't eat an elephant in one bite; you do it one bite at a time." Then, the servant leader assigns those actions to people within the department based on their skills, abilities, and current position. He or she will spend a tremendous amount of time working with each member of the team to ensure everyone understands the strategy, seek their input on how best to implement, and then constantly follow up to ensure they are on track. The servant leader thrives on measuring and metrics. Servant leaders know people love to know the score, so they will develop charts and graphs, showing key metrics and results to the team.

As talked about in earlier chapters, servant leaders hold lots of meetings with their people, both one on one and in group settings. They will discuss the strategy, how it is progressing, and what changes need to be made and why. Constant communication is the key to strategy success in the servant leader's eyes. **Lesson Learned: Show me a vision that is not communicated to the people, and I will show you a company and its people wandering in the desert.**

## STRATEGY AND DAILY DOSE MUST BE TIED TOGETHER

A great strategy that is not communicated to the people has no path to develop the right "daily dose" required to meet the goals and objectives of the plan. Leave out the right communication, and the whole process will fail to produce the results that were planned. I have seen this process fall short many times during my career. We as leadership will go through days of strategic planning meetings, discussing our dreams and plans with lots of enthusiasm and excitement, including lots of flip chart pages, graphs, PowerPoint presentations, and backup for the recommendations presented and discussed. Then, everyone leaves, knowing what they want to accomplish and ready to slay dragons to be successful. But somewhere between the meeting room and next month, it all falls apart or gets delayed. Why?

## BARRIERS TO A SUCCESSFUL STRATEGY

- People get busy working in the business and not on the business.
- The daily "fire drills" start, and working on the future loses out to what is important today.
- People on the manufacturing floor and in the office don't have a clue, because no one communicates to them.
- The business didn't have the right people with the experience needed to bring success.
- Smaller companies find it hard to find the money to invest in the new equipment or new technology they need.
- Then, there's the age-old problem of knowing what to do vs. doing it.

Another year goes by with flat or declining results, while stress and disappointment continue. Where does this process fall down? It falls at the feet of the leaders. I can look back at my own career and see the times I took my own eye off the ball, and we got behind in our strategy communication plan and follow-through. We get so caught up in producing reports for corporate, and we forget about the "blocking and tackling" of the business, which is where real people work every day on the daily dose if the strategy has any chance of succeeding and coming to life. I have never heard of a company that has gone out of business because it didn't produce enough reports or paperwork. Plenty have failed because the communication broke down, the strategy didn't get implemented, and the people didn't know what they needed to do.

## ENSURING SERVANT LEADER PRINCIPLES ARE IN PLACE

Servant leaders bring an atmosphere of community and a sense of unity to their team and the business. People on their team know their goals and objectives and understand the accountability that comes along with the plan. The team was a participant in developing the action plans for their area or department. Servant leaders are not in an office, watching from afar; they are in the battle with their team. They bring encouragement, inspiration, and motivation to help them accomplish their daily dose. They know their people, their skill sets and talents, and who to assign to specific actions and plans. Servant leaders are measuring the results daily, so there are fewer surprises when they see the results. Because they are measuring daily, servant leaders can make adjustments faster when things aren't going well.

Servant leaders are not afraid of change to keep things moving. They listen to their people, because they know those closest to the action have the answers. They believe the key to staying on plan with strategy is:

WHAT        do we need to accomplish?

HOW         will we accomplish it?

WHO         will be accountable for making it happen?

WHEN        will we know we are on or off plan?

## SUCCESSFUL STRATEGY COMES FROM PEOPLE NOT WORDS ON A PAGE OR A BIG MEETING

At the end of the day, business is about leaders, people, strategy, actions, implementation, and accountability for the results. Servant leaders know it starts with people, and that is why it's always their main focus. This idea came to light for me back in the mid-'90s, when we were looking at implementing Lean manufacturing in our company. We did a poor man's Lean (no outside help or consultants) and called it "Improve Process." But in reading the Lean books, one theme kept coming up over and over again: the difference in how US companies saw their people vs. the Japanese companies.

The example they gave had to do with a problem on the manufacturing floor. A person comes running in, telling the leaders about a problem on the plant floor that was causing major issues. The American leaders all gathered in the conference room to talk about what was happening, and they tried to figure out what needed to be done to fix the problem. Now, shift to the Japanese company, and the first thing the leaders did was go to the manufacturing floor to observe the problem themselves and talk with the people, asking for their ideas and suggestions. Obviously, there is a big difference in how each group of leaders reacted. Servant leaders have learned during their leadership journey that being close to the action is where problems get solved, and leaders can make a real difference. **Lesson**

**Learned: Conference rooms are for private meetings, video conferences, and pizza lunches—not for solving problems or developing people.**

One last thought for this chapter. Always remember that when the strategy isn't working and is getting bogged down, go back to the daily dose, and talk with the people closest to the action. They may not always know how to solve the problem, but they can tell you the issues and barriers that are preventing them and the company from making it happen.

# CHAPTER TEN

# SERVANT LEADERS AND MISTAKES

One thing that all leaders will face during their careers is the mistakes and even failures they and their people will deal with. They are caused by:

- Wrong decisions being made based on inaccurate information
- Lack of communication between those who need to make decisions
- Surprises that can occur in the marketplace, with customers, suppliers and competitors, with which you have little or no control
- Waiting too long to make a decision
- Not making a decision at all
- Lack of training
- Poor leadership
- Lack of support from corporate

On and on the list could go. We know that almost all mistakes and failures involve people in some way. People are not perfect, we all make mistakes, and businesses will have to deal with the consequences of those mistakes. Hopefully, the mistakes will be small and not cause terrible consequences for the business or harm to people.

You can tell a lot about a leader or company by how he or she handles mistakes and failure. I have seen some leaders who scream and yell and turn something small into something bigger because of their attitude and reaction. I have seen others who let mistakes go without saying anything and act as though nothing happened. They kind of sweep it under the rug. Both of these types of reactions are wrong and hurt the performance of the company and the people.

But servant leaders see mistakes and failure in a different light. They see them as great learning opportunities, or as some call them, "teachable moments," which create a work environment that helps us learn from our mistakes and work toward making only new mistakes. They try to create an environment where failure is seen as something that happens when people try some great new things, even if they don't work out. **Lesson Learned: Real innovation in business is created by not having a fear of failure.**

Now, I'm not talking about things like people driving forklift trucks 30 mph though a facility or people ignoring safety rules that can result in harm to them or someone else. I'm talking about the day-to-day decisions, where people may try to develop a new product, call on a new prospect, try a new selling technique, make a decision based on the information they have in front of them at the moment, or make a mistake in how they handled a people issue. These are all types of decisions that people—from janitor to president—make every day in their job. Servant leaders will judge someone on their heart, the reason they tried a new task, or a new way of doing something.

There is an old story I heard many years ago about a leader who made a decision that caused his company to take a $1,000,000 loss. He knew he had to go tell his president what he had done and expected to get fired. After telling the president, the leader said, "Well, I guess you are going to fire me."

The president said, "No, I'm not firing you. I just spent $1,000,000 on your education."

Servant leaders know that for a company to prosper, they must create an environment that will accept some mistakes and failures. If people get beat up when they try something new, change will grind to a halt, and the company will be left to live with old ways and systems for accomplishing their work and less innovation. The creative people will leave the company, and those who are happy with the status quo will be all that is left.

When failure happens, servant leaders go into the coaching mode. They try and pick up the person, explaining failure is normal and never to quit. They review with the person why he or she made the decision, what went wrong, and what should be done differently if the individual had it to do all over again. It becomes that teachable moment that servant leaders handle so well with their people and teams.

## HOW SERVANT LEADERS HANDLE FAILURE WITH THEIR PEOPLE

- Help their people see it by teaching, not punishment or embarrassment
- Help their people see innovation and failure go together
- Help them understand that everyone fails, but the strong get back up
- Help their people learn about perseverance
- Help them build trust with their people
- Help open the door to great communication

## WHAT PEOPLE LEARN ABOUT FAILURE FROM A SERVANT LEADER

- They can trust their leader, because they coach and mentor instead of "bark" at them.
- Failure is part of life, and it can make you better and stronger.
- Teachable moments are about getting better and should not to be dreaded.
- They can speak truth to their leader and don't have to hide things.
- Failure is many times a prerequisite for success.

No one sets out in life or business with a mind-set or goal for failure. But failure will find us all during our life's journey. The ability to work through failure and pick ourselves up is where strength and faith are learned and developed. I can look back over my own business career and life and see that I learned so much more from my mistakes and failures than I ever did from my success. Success can make us lazy and even keep us from taking new steps or new directions. We get comfortable and stop reaching for new heights or new direction from God. Failure can also paralyze and keep us from moving forward. Depending on your perspective, failure can be your friend or your enemy. It can provide you with great learning experiences or teach you to fear trying new things.

My failures have helped me stop and look at myself, my decisions, and my motives: to really take an honest look into my heart. Sometimes, I didn't like what I saw, but a loving God, my wife, and some great mentors got me through those times and gave me new perspectives and direction. **Lesson Learned: Failure is not meant to be lived alone.** We need leaders who can come alongside us to give us inspiration and strength. We need a family that can pick us up and give us love—or kick us in the backside when we need a jump-start. But most important, we need a faith in God who created us and gave us unique skills and talents and a path to follow during our journey. Leave out God, and we will get lost; invite him in, and while our journey won't be perfect, God will be right there with us to see us through. He will carry us when we don't have the strength and love us when we need to feel loved.

# CHAPTER ELEVEN

# DEVELOPING CHAMPIONS

Have you ever noticed the excitement that happens when people and companies are planning for a big sales meeting? People are moving heaven and earth to make it happen, no expense is too big, and these meetings are sometimes held at big resorts or fancy hotels. People really get pumped and excited over the whole experience.

Sales meetings are very important, because you need a trained and focused sales force who come together to share their ideas and discuss new product offerings, competitors, pricing, and the many issues and challenges they face maintaining their current customers and developing new ones. As someone who spent a good part of my own career in field sales and then as a regional sales manager, product manager, sales manager, and vice president of sales and marketing, I certainly understand the importance of these meetings.

Now, let's move to the HR department, where the vice president of HR is planning the company's training strategy and budget for the year. It includes a training program for the senior leadership team, middle managers, team leaders, and supervisors. It also has some money built into the budget for some off-site training for individuals to attend meetings to help them improve their job skills and team building. Also, some coaching and mentoring are planned for some of the company's new and future leaders. But there is not a lot of hoopla or excitement going on within the company while these training budgets are being prepared. Not a lot of people are running into HR to ask for more training money or how can they help.

Once the planning is complete, HR presents their training plan and budgets and then start hearing the following: Everyone is busy; should we allow people to have that much time away from their work? Each leader will give a passionate speech about the people they cannot let attend the training because their jobs are too important, and things will slip while they are gone. They will hear that the budget is tight, and they need to cut back on training—but we will do more of it next year. Some leaders and managers will want to know how many people can be eliminated from the list of people to save money, or what training can be eliminated or postponed.

This is a scene that is played out year after year in many companies. I have to admit I have uttered these same words as president, when my HR leaders would bring me their training budgets. We say people are our most important asset and we need our people to improve in their performance, but what actions do we take to make it happen? Do our actions match our talk? Do we get the performance we deserve from our people? Sadly, in many cases, we do not provide the type of consistent training that is needed to improve our results. It's almost like the promise we make to ourselves each year to start an exercise program or new diet. We start out with great enthusiasm and then it dies down. Training is no different. Why is it we can't implement the training we all say is so important to improving our business and our people? What message does it send to our people when we postpone training or scratch them off the list of people who will receive training? We keep telling them they are not performing up to our standards, but how do we help them improve? What is our responsibility as leaders to help our people keep improving?

Can you imagine the football team showing up for practice at the beginning of the season at Notre Dame, and Coach Kelly says, "We are eliminating training and practice. You all have been playing football for many years, so you are as good as you are ever going to be. So, go back to the dorms. Just show up on Saturdays for the game. Here is the playbook; read it, and be prepared for the games. You will have to figure out how to train yourselves, provide your own resources for training, but we expect you to win every game. Take care, and see you Saturday."

Sounds absurd, doesn't it? But, that is what leaders are telling their people when they don't provide training, or only provides them a few hours of training each year. Basically, we are telling them we think they are not going to get any better and just show up to work and it will all work itself out. But we still expect continuous improvement every year. How will we make it happen if we are not training ourselves and our people? The best runners in the world, the ones who hold world records, practice and train hours upon hours every day to run a race that will last around ten seconds in the hundred-yard dash. What does that say about the importance of training? I think it speaks volumes.

## WHY IS TRAINING IMPORTANT

- Helps leaders improve their skills, learn new ones, and understand the company's expectations for leadership
- Puts feet to our, "People are our most important asset"
- Helps us to accomplish our goals throughout all levels of our organization
- Helps us spot winners; training helps them stand out
- Helps align people with our strategies
- Ensures everyone is on the same page
- Helps motivate and inspire people
- Helps our people develop and improve their skills
- Develops best practices and shares knowledge
- Helps people know how to do their work better
- Provides a systematic and organized process for improvement
- Helps build a culture of learning and improvement
- Tells our people that we really do care about helping them reach their potential

## WHERE TO SPEND YOUR TRAINING DOLLARS

### Servant Leadership Training

Leaders set the rhythm for the company, develop the strategy for the future, influence and encourage the people, and set the expectations. Who is helping them grow as leaders and to reach their leadership potential, to learn how to communicate, resolve conflict, and prepare the associates for a future that is always changing? Without servant leadership training, where will our leaders learn how to work with their peers as a team and eliminate the jealousy that will crop up between them? How will they learn how to teach to make a difference in people's lives? We need to remember that leaders always take the company and its people down a path. Without consistent training and leadership, and establishment of leadership expectations, where will they take your company? Do you know, and is it where you want it to go?

## Middle Managers and Supervisors

This is the group that has the biggest impact on the way day-to-day operations of any business work and how people get their work done. They deliver the message of senior leadership to the people. Do they know how to communicate, encourage, and motivate your people? Do they listen, ask for feedback, set goals and priorities, and help their people achieve the right results? If you asked your people what they thought about this group, what would they say? What would they say needs to improve in their leadership styles and actions? It is by far the most untrained and in need of training group within any company. Most got their promotion because they were good at doing things like maintenance, sales, running a machine, or a good accountant. Who taught them to be a leader? How many hours do they spend in training per year? Is it enough to bring about real change?

## Team Leaders

These are up-and-comers who are working to move into supervision. Do they get the training needed to take that next step? Are they being trained by people who need lots of training themselves? Do you know what their weaknesses are and in what areas they need training? Do they understand the expectations for them? Are they leading or pulling their people? Did they get this job because they were good potential leaders, or because they could do things well with their hands? Who is teaching them leadership principles? How will they get better?

## Sales Force and Customer Service

Serving customers is a high calling. This group takes the personality and value proposition of your company to your markets, customers, and prospects. How do your customers perceive it? Customers vote every day with how they think you are meeting their needs with their purchase orders.

Who is training this group in value-added selling and partnership selling, or as I call it, understanding your customers' problems and pain? If there was ever a need for servant leadership it is in the sales area. Can you imagine the business you could receive if customers really looked at your sales team as a "servant sales team" who put their customers first? Have they been trained in developing solutions that meet your customers' needs? Who is going to help sales and engineering learn how to work better together and break down those walls that have always excited between sales, manufacturing, and engineering? How often does the training occur? Just during a sales meeting? Who follows up to ensure the training is making a difference in the results?

## The Entire Workforce

Everyone in a company needs ongoing training to learn how to improve in their job. It's not too complicated. If we truly want to create an environment of continuous improvement, we need to be about training the people who do the work: training in problem solving, how to communicate with each other, team building, resolving conflict, and improving their skills to achieve continuous improvement for themselves and the company. Help them discover their potential by creating ways for them to try new things and be innovative. Create a learning environment where people and ideas can flourish.

## THE FOLLOW-UP AFTER TRAINING

Who is going to follow up to see if the training is working? Are people improving? Have metrics been established to see if training is making a difference in the way people work together, and are the company results improving because of training? Will coaching and mentoring programs be provided? Who will be the coaches, and are they capable? Will training be a once or twice a year event or a way of life?

Do you remember in the second chapter the description of a servant leader's vision? If not, here it is again:

**The best strategy to achieve organizational goals and create competitive advantage is by developing an environment of caring, mutual trust, and respect between the leaders and the people by focusing their strategy on developing the full potential of all associates and the business, therefore creating a winning partnership.**

As you read this vision again, hopefully you will see that training would be a major component of how a servant leader would create this type of organization. Training is a core need for everyone, in every company, and how a servant leader helps implement their vision and develop the foundation needed for success.

Through my own business experience, both good and bad, I truly believe training offers the best opportunity for a business to create a company with a winning competitive advantage for their people and the business. I know it sounds so simple and easy, yet very few companies use training to its fullest potential. We tend to look at training as an event or something we have to do to meet some ISO or Lean quality requirement.

Most leaders fail not because they don't have potential but because they aren't ready and haven't been trained with a plan or a leadership growth process in mind. No one sits down with them and asks, "What do you believe your weaknesses are and how can I help you?" They are thrown into the lion's den (willingly) and expected to be ready for battle. They would never admit to not being ready, because that wouldn't be good for their careers. They believe that because they now have a title, all they have to do is tell people what to do, and it will be done; that their authority will rule, instead of understanding that titles don't work anymore. And if they do, it only works for a short period of time. Influence, and the right kind of influence, is what will make or break them as a leader.

If you really want to change your organization and create and model the behavior and vision of a servant leader, I urge you to make training your number-one strategy going forward; spend money on training like you mean it and your people and business depends on it, because they do. I believe the lack of a real leadership training process is leaving many leaders stressed and feeling inadequate and at a loss for how to lead today's diverse and capable workforce. Many leaders would rather blame it on the "workers are lazy and hard to find" excuse we seem to use way too often. Lack of an effective training process is leaving many potential servant leaders in the dust, as the world passes them and their companies behind. If companies can truly be committed to building a repeatable and sustainable process, which is given the time and money needed to succeed it will change the company, its leaders, and their people forever.

Let your competitors spend many sleepless nights trying to figure out how you are gaining a competitive advantage in the marketplace. They will never figure it out!

# CHAPTER TWELVE

# THE TEN P'S

I know I have really confused you with this title. Even my wife said I must have lost it, since I'm getting to the end of writing my book. In trying to sum up who a servant leader is, what he or she stands for, and a servant leader thinks, I developed what I call the "Ten-P Formula." I know, it sounds kind of silly. But for me, it's a way for everyone to understand and remember what servant leaders are all about: what drives them, how do they lead, and what can happen when they are allowed to bring these strengths, skills, and traits to business and people. All the words that I chose to describe the servant leader begin with P, thus the reason or the name the Ten-P Formula.

## 1. Purpose

When I refer to purpose in my book, it is describing what God intended for each of our lives: a plan that God purposed for every single individual he has created. One of my favorite scriptures explains it very well.

15 My frame was not hidden from you
when I was made in the secret place,
when I was woven together in the depths of the earth.
16 Your eyes saw my unformed body;
all the days ordained for me were written in your book
before one of them came to be.
Psalm 139:15–16 (NIV)

God is and has been involved in every aspect of our lives, before we were created and still today. He created us because he loves us and wants to have a relationship with us. A relationship where he pours out that love in our lives, and we then share that love with the people he places in our lives. He poured out his love, grace, and mercy when he sent his son, Jesus Christ, to show us what real love was all about. He then showed us an even greater example of love when Jesus went to the cross to die for our sins. Because of this sacrifice, those who accept Christ as the Savior and repent of their sins can have eternal life with God. Because of Jesus's sacrifice of love and mercy, we are called to impact the lives of people during our life's journey.

God created each of us with the skills, abilities, talents, and personality to find the purpose he ordained for us and to support that purpose and journey, as we put into practice our purpose and faith. We are all perfectly made to fulfill the purpose God has called us accomplish.

Our journey is one where we discover, develop, and become the person God created us to be. Many of us will struggle with finding our purpose as we travel life's journey, and sadly, some will never find it. As I wrote earlier, I didn't start discovering my own purpose until I was in my thirties, and even though I found it, I still struggle with staying on course each and every day. Staying on track is a constant battle for most of us because of our selfish tendencies and the pull the world has on us. Our greed, hunger for power, selfishness, and our goals are all desired based on our timetable. We start thinking we know what's best for our lives versus what God, the creator, has planned. We become like teenagers going through puberty, thinking we have all the answers.

I believe God is constantly trying to get our attention by showing us how the world's lure can tear apart our lives and isn't the answer for true happiness and success. All we have to do is read the newspaper or watch TV almost daily to see the many so-called successful businesspeople, athletes, politicians, actors, musicians, and yes, even some religious leaders, who have fallen. They seemed to have it all: money, fortune, fame, beautiful homes, cars, beautiful spouses, and great careers. Yet, it could not satisfy them, as they wanted more and more of everything. What they thought was success actually changed their lives and plans, and in some cases, ruined their lives and those of their family and many others. They thought they had found their purpose and passion, but it was all false and blew away like paper in a windstorm. When God is not at the center of our lives, and we are not seeking his will and purpose for our lives, we will try and fill that void with the many things that look so great but can destroy us and bring us many of the struggles we face in our lives.

Finding our purpose requires us to trust, grow in our faith, overcome our fears, and build a discipline that keeps us grounded. Why? Because, when God comes knocking on our door with opportunities and new paths for us to travel, we will have to conquer our fears and follow him. If not, we will fall further behind in our search for our purpose, and we will travel many paths that God did not intend for us. Or God will have to, as my pastor recently said, put us in a timeout for our own good and protection.

I have shared the many times God moved us as a family during my career. At the time, I thought it was about the new jobs and all about God blessing me. It was God really building my faith and trust in him, my growth as a servant leader, and the people that God put in my life. I shudder sometimes to think where I might be if we had said no to God when he was stirring in our hearts during those times. With that said, I know there have been times when I said no to God and turned toward the world and all I thought it had to offer. The purpose-filled life—while filled with potholes, struggles, and mistakes—brings a joy that only God can bring by our loving and serving him and taking that love and caring and sharing it with the people he puts into our lives. Learn to enjoy the journey.

## 2. Passion

Once you have discovered your purpose, you will spend time trying to find where and how to fulfill God's purpose in your life. Since our purpose is driven by our relationship with God, it means you are called to impact the lives of people we meet during our life's journey. Then, our passion will be about serving people in some way. It can happen in just about any career or volunteer position we might choose in life. Remember, your purpose is to show Christ to those we meet by building relationships based on caring for people and impacting their lives in a positive way. Your passion will take you down the avenue you choose to carry out your purpose.

For purposes of my book, I'm talking about servant leaders, whose purpose is to care for and impact the lives of people in a positive way. Their passion is to accomplish that purpose in their role as leaders in a business environment. To help people be all they can be based on God's wisdom and truth. Servant leaders are passionate about the success of their people and the company for which they work. They realize that if they can build a caring environment, where people can thrive and reach their potential, the business will be successful in creating security for the people and the company, creating a shared partnership of mutual respect, trust, and success.

Other people who have discovered their purpose may find their passion teaching in schools, as a nurse, doctor, secretary, housewife, coach, serving in ministry as a career or volunteer, a parent, and many other roles in life that can impact others' lives in a supportive and caring way. The list is endless.

## 3. People

People are at the heart of every servant leader's purpose and passion. They realize that to God, people really are the most important asset, and we are called into a partnership with God to accomplish his mission of caring for and impacting the lives of the people he puts in our path.

As a servant leader, it means seeing people as the most important asset in a company. I have often thought of the time and money we spend in business on preventive maintenance on our machines and the upkeep of our buildings, trucks, IT equipment, and many other assets. Yet, we find it hard to spend even five to ten minutes with our people a day or two a week. I'm talking about "real time," where we are talking with them person to person, understanding their needs and goals, and learning how we can help them reach their potential. It's about getting past the surface and getting to know the person and his or her heart.

Many leaders hesitate to talk with their people this way, not because they are bad leaders, but because they have never been trained in how to or the importance of building that kind of relationship. Has anyone ever discussed the expectation for them as a leader? Do companies really see it as important for their leaders to build those kinds of relationships with their people? In many cases during my career, I have known leaders who felt it would make them seem weak as a leader if they built relationships. Or, they might become too close to their people, making it hard for them to lead or make tough decisions.

I think we have to get rid of that kind of thinking if we really want to create a caring environment and harness the talent, skills, and innovation of our people to achieve great things. I do not believe work is something that we should separate from life, relationships, and caring for people. As I discussed earlier, it's where we spend most of the time we are awake. So, why shouldn't we make it an exciting, caring, relationship-building part of our life? I know I'm just a country boy from Virginia, but I know one thing: people who are trained and led by caring, results-oriented leaders will be happier and will always produce better results than people working in an uncaring workplace, where leaders give them very little training or help. It's that simple.

## 4. Principles

Every servant leader I have ever met is led by certain principles in their life. These principles stay with them no matter where they go or what career path they might choose. While these principles may change as they grow older and mature in wisdom, they usually help the leader to become even more caring and people focused.

These principles begin forming in our early years and start to take hold as we begin making our own decisions. The people in your life during your early years will also have an impact on your principles, which can be good and bad. When I look at my own journey, I was very blessed to have parents who had a very positive impact on my life and truly modeled the way servant leaders should lead and live life. They modeled the Golden Rule: "Do unto others as you would have them do unto you." While I have to admit that I didn't always follow their wise advice and counsel, it is and has always been part of my internal compass. I shudder to think what might have been if I had not had this great beginning in my life. Even with that great start, I was very selfish, and life was all about me during my younger years. Without that great start from my parents, I believe my life could have easily gone in a different direction and one that would have sent me down a path that would have brought me great disappointment and discontent.

Too often without strong guiding principles in a leader's life, he or she can go down a path of greed, searching for power and all they can get. I can truly attest to the fact that if your guiding principles are modeled after the Golden

Rule, your life will be one of greater joy and happiness. Yes, there will be disappointments and failure, but you will be better prepared to handle them and have the strength and ability to pick yourself up to start a new day.

As a servant leader, your principals are guided by the following main elements:

- You have a caring heart for people.
- You desire to impact positively the lives of the people who God sends into your life.
- You understand the principle of stewardship, which simply put, means whatever God has entrusted and blessed you with—family, job, and the people you are leading, a business where you serve as a leader, money, and possessions are all managed with great care.
- You see the positives and potential in people.
- You build your relationships with people around encouragement, caring, motivation, and the discipline for doing what is right for the right reasons.
- Your foundation for your principles is built around your faith and relationships with God and his son, Jesus Christ.
- You realize you are not perfect and don't have all the answers to life and people.

Principles are what help people and businesses succeed. If your principles are not strong, you will be blown around like a tree in a strong storm, moving from side to side. Let your guiding principles be based on God's truth of:

- Mercy and grace
- Having a discipline in life for doing the right things for the right reasons
- Accountability for the actions we take
- Being a good steward for that which has been entrusted to us
- Caring for people
- Knowing love is the greatest commandment.

## 5. Potential

Servant leaders get excited about the potential they see in people. It's one of the differences in servant leaders versus other types of leaders. Servant leaders talk about the potential of their people, while other leaders talk more about their people's weaknesses. Servant leaders start looking for the potential in their people the minute they first meet someone they will be leading. They also don't judge people based on their looks, background, and education. The people they lead start with a clean sheet of paper and lots of opportunities.

During my first day as president at the last company where I held that position, I had a very unusual situation happen with one of the salespeople. I had scheduled meetings with all the salespeople, senior managers, supervisors, and key people at the headquarters plant. This was to give them a chance to meet with me one on one and time to express their thoughts on the state of the company and the issues and challenges they were facing in their departments. When I met with one of the salespeople, the first thing out of his mouth was if several things did or did not happen, he was going to quit. No hello or how are you. Well, as you can imagine, this was a first for me as a leader. But I guess growing up in the mountains of Virginia gave me the ability to not be too surprised at life, so I softly said, "Nice to meet you. Why don't you sit down for a few minutes, and let's talk before you quit."

Well, two hours later after some very honest conversation, he left my office still employed. What I had seen was a person with lots of spirit, a passion for succeeding, and a fire in his belly to prove he could do the job. What he needed was a leader who could give him some guidance, support, and a dose of reality and honesty. We built a great relationship during the coming months, and about a year later, I promoted him to sales manager for one of our product lines. He did a great job and grew the product line from around $500,000 in annual sales to over $6 million in a little over two years. What I saw was someone with lots of passion and potential, while leaders before me saw a troublemaker, who kept trying to get them to listen to his ideas and suggestions. I would agree that his tact at times wasn't the best, but what leaders do is train and teach others how to improve and make adjustments in how they work and deal with people. The prior leaders just didn't know how or didn't want to spend the time and effort needed to harness his energy. The key for this success was the building of our relationship, which opened the door for us to trust, understand, and talk openly about any subject.

There are lots of people like this in the business world: people with passion, heart, and energy, who just need someone to come alongside of them and say, "Hey, I know you have some great ideas. How can I help you succeed?" Do all situations like this work out as well as this one did? No. But it could work out a lot better if leaders would drop their big-title attitudes and build relationships with their people, find out what makes them tick, their goals, what gets them excited, and how they can help them.

There is so much potential passing though the doors of every company every day that is going untapped. People who want to accomplish great things for their families are just looking for some leader to give them a hand, to show some attention, ask for their ideas and suggestions, and then give them the tools to succeed. What are we waiting on?

## 6. Planning

In business and life, planning is one of the most important tools and exercises anyone can go through. Good planning starts with a destination in mind. Without that, you don't know what to plan for. If I came home and said to my wife, "We are going on vacation in two weeks. Be ready," I would get that look that says; "You've got to be kidding me, right?" She would want to know:

- Where are we going?
- How much is it going to cost?
- What's the weather like this time of year?
- What type of clothes should we take?
- When are we leaving and then coming home?
- Are we flying or driving?
- Where are we staying?
- Are we going by ourselves or with another couple?
- Is it all fun or mixed with business?

On and on the questions would fly rapid fire, all legitimate and that need to be answered.

Something like this happens in businesses every day, when a president walks into a conference room filled with leaders and says, "We are going to grow our business and profits by 20 percent this year." Setting goals is the easy part. Meeting those goals and planning how we will achieve them is the hard part.

In business, we are eager to set goals, because that's what leaders do. It makes us feel good to lay out strategy. But in my humble opinion, the most important part of the process is the planning of the people side of strategy: what people resources are needed, the qualifications and skill levels needed, how many people will be needed, and where and when. This is usually skipped over or just touched on, because it is the hardest part. Can you imagine the army setting a strategy to go to war and leaving out the people resource needs and what tools they will need to be successful? It wouldn't happen, because military leaders know victory is achieved with people. Business is not any different. **Lesson Learned: Success is driven by having the right people, in the right positions, at the right time and accomplishing the right things.**

Discussing the people side of planning and strategy requires us to face our people issues and failures as leaders. In many cases, we have done a poor job in training and developing our people, causing the shortfall in meeting our goals and strategies, and a shortfall in the talent needed to take our strategy forward. That's when the famous, "Our people are no good or lazy," speeches are heard in conference rooms. **Lesson Learned: When people fail in their jobs, it is almost always a failure of leadership.** We need to stop looking for a place to lay the blame other than on ourselves.

Servant leaders are constantly planning, but the most important part of their planning has to deal with people. They are trying to determine:

- What daily dose of actions is needed for their people to meet their goals, and what people skills are needed to make it happen?
- What are the gaps in people skills and abilities needed to meet their goals?
- What training needs to be established, how often, and who needs to participate to improve and develop the skills needed?
- Are there any gaps in their people needs? If so, do they need to add people with those skill sets?
- What training processes are needed for the future that will help develop their people and get them ready for the future?

I have tried to make sure that as you read my book, (I'm sure you got that hint by now) that success in business starts and ends with people: those who do the work. Planning is no exception. Always be thinking about the people side of planning at the beginning of the strategic planning process, not at the end. At the end, it's too late!

## 7. Priorities

The setting of priorities is probably one of the most important skills leaders can develop for themselves and their people. They know that leadership is really a balancing act between how leaders spend their time with people, doing tasks, planning, actions, and in what order. Servant leaders see the setting of priorities as key to not only leading their people effectively but also in managing their own personal lives to ensure they stay grounded in their principles. They know that it is easy to let life get away from you and start setting your priorities based on your wants versus setting your priorities based on the purpose God established for you.

A servant leader's number-one priority when it comes to leading his or her people in business is caring for and impacting the people's lives God puts in his or her path, so the people and the company can maximize their potential and results. To accomplish and meet this priority requires servant leaders:

- To develop relationships with the people they lead
- To understand their people's needs, skills, goals, and potential
- To focus on and spend real time with their people; one-on-one listening, giving and receiving feedback, and acting on what they learned about their people
- To develop an improvement plan for their people's training and skill improvement
- To develop a written plan with priorities for their people that is shared so they understand where they are headed and there is a plan for their improvement
- To ensure people understand the goals and strategies of the company and how they each can and will impact the results by their actions
- To establish accountability for the result with their people and themselves

Priority setting is also how servant leaders keep their personal lives moving in the right direction. It's how they stay away from the lure of the world's definition of success. The drivers of their personal priorities are:

- God
- Family
- Caring for the people God put in their path
- Continually learning, reading, and improving themselves

Priorities are something at which we must continually work. There are many distractions in our lives, both at work and outside of work, which can easily get us off track. Stay grounded in you purpose, passion, God, family, and other people's needs, and you will be able to fight the good fight and keep life's distractions under control.

## 8. Persuasion

Most servant leaders are very good at persuading people to follow them, not because they are just good with words, but because they are real and build trust with their people one moment and action at a time. People want to be led by honest, caring, knowledgeable, leaders who help them accomplish things they never thought possible; leaders who spend time with them listening to their issues, struggles, goals, hopes and dreams.

Too often, leaders fail not because they are not capable of being a good leader but because they don't spend time with their people and their people don't get to know them. These types of leaders have been trained to always have their game face on and never let people see the real person who also has dreams, goals, and fears—just like the people they lead. **Lesson Learned: True servant leadership is about sharing life with the people you lead. It's not done successfully stranger to stranger.**

If you want to have influence with your people as a leader, you must first:

- Care for your people and let them see and feel it.
- Let them see the real you—warts and all.
- Let them know you don't have all the answers, and you need their help.
- Communicate, communicate, and communicate. There is never too much.

- Ask for their opinion.
- Tell them you appreciate them, and more important, show that appreciation.
- Train and teach them.
- Set expectations and then help them reach them.
- Don't be a stranger; be seen and heard in person
- The icing on the cake is really getting to know them.

Persuasion, the kind that moves people and companies to new directions and develops sustainable success, comes from positive actions that impact people's lives. **Lesson Learned: It does not come from carrying a big stick or with a title.**

## 9. Partners

Servant leaders have learned during their life's journey that people were meant to share and do life together. Life without relationships and people is lonely. Servant leaders also understand that relationships in business and between leaders and the people they lead are no different. If a company wants to build a sustainable competitive advantage, it will take people working together with shared values, goals, and purpose to make it happen. It will also require leaders who understand the principle of relationships and doing life together, and leading to make it come alive.

Somehow, we have told ourselves in business that if people are talking, they are not working, that the workplace should be a place where people keep their heads down, only speak if spoken to by their leader, and look up only when the whistle blows or it's time to go home. Successful servant leader driven companies of today like Southwest Airlines, Aflac, Starbucks, Chick-fil-A, Marriott,WD-40 and Herman Miller to name a few, are leaders in innovation and change, because they understand how to get people to work together. They know for innovation and success to take place, it requires their people and leadership to work together in new ways to tap the collective ability and potential of their people. They turn people loose to try new things, be creative, and ask lots of questions of themselves, their coworkers, and their leaders.

We should turn away from using the old terms, like, "labor," and "hourly workers," and begin using the term "partners or associates." Start using a word that brings dignity and helps to remind us of the relationships that are needed to create the competitive advantage needed to survive.

If a business can create this kind of partnership, its problems with turnover and recruiting new people would almost disappear. People would be lined up in the parking lot, trying to get hired. Customers would be lined up to purchase your products and services, because you would be more innovative, cost effective, and offer better quality than your competitors. You would have a true competitive advantage created by everyone in your company. Now that is a true partnership!

## 10. Perseverance

Without perseverance, many servant leaders would have given up on their journey early in life. Most servant leaders have a story to tell. First, servant leaders are not and have never been perfect. Many of them a have gone down paths in their life they probably wished they had not traveled: paths that created scars and hurts, but also paths that taught them some valuable lessons about themselves, people, and life. These are paths that God allows us to travel to teach us valuable lessons about life and to help us find our purpose and passion in life.

In my own life, I can point to paths I traveled that gave me a new perspective about life and showed me that I was wandering away from what God intended for me and my life. These paths were leading me to selfishness, and as I described earlier, that "it's all about me syndrome." Luckily the lessons my parents had taught me in my early years, along with pastors who impacted me, kept me from wandering too far off the path. But like a teenager who keeps testing their parents, I kept testing God. But he was faithful, gave me mercy and grace when I didn't deserve any, and sent people into my life that got me back on track.

Perseverance is a funny thing. **Lesson Learned: I think you sometimes have to be on the brink of giving up before finding and making perseverance your friend.** That is the moment when you have tried everything, nothing is working, people aren't listening to you as a leader, you wonder if it is all worth it, and you are just about ready to give up and quit. Then, that special something kicks in that doesn't let you give up. It gives you a new energy, new thoughts, and eyes to see the possibilities.

You remember the people who count on you and need you to help them reach their potential.

Perseverance is also needed by servant leaders, because their journey is not always an easy one. People will question your ideas and ways of leading. At times, people will think you are soft and not tough enough to lead. Leading to make a difference and build a sustainable competitive advantage is about long-term thinking, and many companies are always in their short-term thinking mode because of their financial shape and needs. Your leadership principles and strategies will put you at odds with this style of company. But you must persevere, because these companies that get into their short-term thinking mode have not solved the problems and issues they deal with every day, year after year. They never take the time to build the foundation that can create the sustainable success and results they need and want.

Perseverance says, "I trust God and there is a reason I am at this company or going through this tough season in my life. Then when—and if—it is time for me to go in another direction, he will open the doors wide and give me the ride of my life." Enjoy the journey and the people he places in your life, for God will use them to impact your life and bring you great joy and contentment.

# CHAPTER THIRTEEN

# HR NEEDS A STRONGER VOICE

If there was ever a group in senior leadership who deserve better treatment and more respect for the job they do, it is HR leaders and their department. In many companies, they are sometimes treated like second-class citizens. We need to change our views on HR and see them as an integral part of all our strategies, because all strategies start and end with people.

We need to give HR the same respect we would give to the sales and marketing department. We tell ourselves our sales department is the voice of the customer in our companies, so HR needs to be looked at as the "voice of the people" in our companies; those people we claim are our most important asset.

The HR department and its leaders need to be viewed as the *people experts* within our company. But many times, we give them so many other duties it makes it hard for them to do the things they need to accomplish to keep the focus on people. Especially in smaller companies or divisions, where we ask HR to wear many different hats, taking their time away from working on the many people issues and strategies that need their attention. Most of the HR people I have been around never complain about taking on these extra duties, because they are about helping the company any way they can. They truly care about the company and helping it become successful.

Here are some examples of how we treat our HR leaders:

- We ask them to pick up or call in the sandwich order for our leadership meetings.
- Sometimes, senior leadership meetings are held, and the HR leader isn't invited.
- We give them duties like keeping up with safety records, OSHA, managing the cleaning people, and picking up things people need.
- When they come to us with their training budget, we ask them to reduce the cost and take some people off the list.
- We blame them for turnover and absenteeism problems, or why we can't recruit good people. Then, when they explain the reasons to us, we won't listen or make the changes needed.

If companies really want to change their culture and create an environment where people are being trained and reaching their potential and leadership is growing in their skills and ability to lead, HR needs to be looked at as a strategic partner to all groups and leaders within the company.

My recommendation is that HR needs to report to the president of the company, especially if it is a smaller company or one with only one location. If HR is a corporate function within a larger company, it should definitely report to the president or, at a minimum, a high-ranking senior vice president.

If you think about all that is going on in our business world today, HR needs to play a very important role. Some of the major issues companies are dealing with that impact the people and culture are:

- Layoffs, terminations, reduction in pay and benefits, reduction in the hours people are working
- Stressed workers, managers, and leaders, who are being asked to do more with less
- Retention of talent when people are feeling as though the company doesn't care anymore
- High turnover and employee dissatisfaction in spite of high unemployment
- Declining morale within the workforce
- The need for more leadership training to help leaders learn how to lead in the new normal, while training budgets are decreased or eliminated

- Diversity of today's workforce, with different nationalities, languages, age differences, and skill levels
- Rising cost of health benefits and insurance

When you look at this list, you can easily see how each and every one of these issues and challenges can and does have a dramatic impact on the strategies and results of every company today, no matter their size. So, if companies want to deal effectively with these issues, HR needs to be seen as a strategic partner by every department and every leader. This needs to be a stated strategy that is communicated to everyone by the company president.

But anyone who has been in business knows that leaders will react to this relationship with HR in different ways. Some leaders do not want any assistance (their word interference) when they are developing people strategies and plans for their people and departments. Others will appreciate having someone who can help them deal with the people issues and needed strategies. Senior leadership must support this initiative, or it will die of its own free will. Why? Because people are busy being busy, and working with another department or additional people requires them to get their work done with someone with different ideas and working style. They will complain it will slow them down, or they don't have time.

If you really want to develop a servant leadership culture, where people really do feel like they are the most important asset and leaders are helping their people discover and reach their potential, HR must take a major leadership role if it is to succeed. HR needs to help:

- Evaluate the current leadership team as to training needs for skill development and improvement.
- Develop and help implement the strategy that helps the company discover and develop the potential of their people (the most underutilized asset in the whole company).
- Develop and implement the strategies to help leaders focus on people and not tasks.
- Evaluate outside training, coaching, and mentoring resources to help with the leadership training and transformation of the total workforce.
- Develop training curriculum and schedules for the training courses.

- Develop budgets and timelines for implementation of the strategy.
- Work with senior leadership in building your strategic model for people improvement.
- Develop tracking programs for measuring results.
- Track people and the training courses they have taken and need to take.

Obviously, there are many more steps, but this helps you get a feel for what needs to be planned and implemented to get started. The success of developing and implementing this process will be dependent on several things:

- Support by the company president first and then all of senior leadership is a must. Without them, it won't work or survive.
- Middle management needs to be on board, or they can kill it because of their daily contact with people, especially in a manufacturing environment.
- Communication with the total workforce is critical. They need to understand what is taking place and help everyone stay committed to the process.
- Once you start the process, you cannot quit, because if you do, the people will see leadership as faking it when it comes to caring about people and creating a workplace where people are the most important asset.

The purpose of this chapter was to make one very important point: HR must be the voice of the people in a valley where there is so much communication clutter and busy being busy taking place that it is hard to get the people message through and implemented. But HR must never stop trying to help leadership understand that business is really all about people. Without people, nothing happens; and with the wrong kind of people, or people who feel the company treats them like warm bodies, lots of things can happen. And most of them are bad.

If a company really does want to achieve maximum results, it must start with helping its people discover and develop their potential. Then, it requires leadership to develop a caring environment, where they are working with their people to achieve great things through encouragement, motivation, and modeling the behavior they want to see in their people.

HR must lead the charge and never give up. They need to take their skills and knowledge of the workforce and make it come alive for the senior leadership, so they know what is really happening outside their doors each and every day.

Senior leadership, you need to let the people in HR do they job they were hired to do: help you manage, lead, and develop the people who come through your doors every day to work. Listen to HR when they tell you about the morale issues that are getting in the way of the company achieving better results. Listen when they tell you about managers and leaders who need help or aren't getting the job done in leading people. Listen to them when they bring you their recommendations for training courses that people need. Give them the training budgets they need to make a difference in people's lives and the company's results. The next time there is a meeting and you need to bring in lunch, ask yourself if you would ask one of your other senior managers to go get it. If not, don't ask HR. Let them spend their time on the people issues that are so important to the success of every company on the planet.

Last, but not least, think about the number-one problem in almost every business today: knowing what they need to do to make their business better, but they never really make the changes needed to make it happen. They are busy working in the business and not on the business.

Remember one important thing: people are your most important asset. So what do you need to start, change, and complete to make your people and business come alive and improve your results? It's never too late to start. Now, go do it!

# CHAPTER FOURTEEN

# FINAL THOUGHTS

When we look at the state of our economic climate, politics, and the decline in trust people around the world have for their leaders, it's easy to see there needs to be a new direction and emphasis on the right kind of leadership. Why? Because, as the old saying goes, "If the results you are getting aren't meeting your goals and expectations, it's insane to keep doing the same old thing."

Almost every night on TV, we see the despair people feel around the world because leadership isn't working. In countries where leaders have used the power of the "big stick and control" leadership model to try and control their people, we see individuals willing to die in the streets to bring about change. In the United States, politicians are finding the old way of leading by creating new spending programs and trying to satisfy special interest groups and be all things to all people isn't working either. People aren't buying their speeches anymore, and the old way of spending our way to prosperity won't work, because the piggybank is empty. The way our politicians have been spending money to make things better is like saying if you need to lose weight, the best way to accomplish that goal is to just keep eating more, and maybe it will work itself out someday.

Today, politicians are into protecting their own ideas and political parties by trying to eliminate real debate or new ideas and thoughts from getting through. Good leadership is about working to eliminate conflict through good communication, listening to other people's ideas, and being civil in the way we treat those with ideas we don't agree with, so we can reach agreement for the good of the people we lead. In my sixty-two years, I have never seen a time in our country where we have so many leaders so out of touch with the people they are leading. It seems leaders today are more driven by their own selfishness, dreams, ideas, and agenda, leaving, "We the people," wondering if it will ever get better. People are already talking about future generations, who will have to lower their expectations for the way life is going to be.

Leaders are forgetting that leadership is *always* about the people. That doesn't mean people will always get what they want, because sometimes it will take a *"new"* medicine to heal what ails us. We found that out as children, when the medicine we took to heal us didn't always taste good but made us feel better. We need leaders who really care about us, who will be honest, explain what needs to be done, and tell us the pain and the sacrifices we must go through and the actions needed to make things better. We need leaders who can develop a three-year strategy, instead of throwing abandon to the wind and coming up with a new program almost every day to satisfy special interests and try to give us false hope.

So, now that I'm off my high horse, let's get back to business leaders and with what they are struggling. The business world has changed and continues to change rapidly. The old paradigms that many of us as leaders were used to are no longer working like they once did, which means leaders must find new ways to lead their people and companies. The power and obedience leadership model needs to be replaced with the caring, motivating, encouraging, and building relationships model. When people ask me why, my answer always is the same: "Which kind of leader would you rather be led by: one who demands, controls, and puts themselves first, or one who encourages, listens, and asks for your opinion, and is constantly working to build a relationship with you?" I think we all know the answer. Now, we need to convince leadership that is the path that needs to be taken.

Let's take a little deeper look at the issues and struggles with which businesses and their leaders must deal.

## BUSINESSES AND LEADERS ARE STRUGGLING TO

- Find new strategies to be competitive in a global economy.
- Develop a consistent strategy that works during tough and uncertain times.
- Deal with the tightening of credit by financial institutions.
- Lead a very diverse workforce (ages, nationalities, languages, and skill levels).
- Deal with the uncertainty of future government regulations and tax laws.
- Find good people in spite of high unemployment rates (their belief).
- Lead with very little in the way of leadership training.
- Overcome the stress and frustrations brought on by working more with less and watching their business struggle and deal with both the joy and heartaches that comes with leadership.

## THE WORKFORCE IS STRUGGLING WITH

- Layoffs, less hours, terminations, reduced pay and benefits, and declining 401K plans.
- How to work with leaders they are losing respect and trust in.
- Being scared for their jobs and an uncertain future for them and their families.
- Having to work longer than planned, because they cannot retire due to their financial situation.
- Being unhappy with where they work and their perception of how they are treated by an uncaring leadership.

So, what we have are the leaders of a company and their workforce (their most important asset) all stressed and frustrated, and because of these struggles, a gap has developed between them that hurts how they work with each other and impacts the results of the business. When stress, frustration, and distrust develop in any relationship—whether a business, marriage, or with a best friend—things have a tendency to go downhill quickly.

How do we stop this spiral and get relationships back on track in our businesses and with our people? How can we get everyone to see through the everyday clutter that takes place in business and understand we truly need each other if our business is going to survive and prosper? What kind of leadership is needed to bring about the changes we desperately need? What is the best way for these two groups to understand they need to come together to create a competitive advantage that creates security for the workforce, leadership, and the business? Who will help them find that path and, more important, bring the encouragement, motivation, energy, and right motives to keep everyone focused and traveling on their journey together?

## To Develop This Type of Business Environment Requires Several Things

- Businesses must learn to embrace the vision and principles that servant leaders bring to a business and the people who work there. They must ask themselves what is the best way of leading: carrying a big stick and pushing and pulling, or building true caring relationships with the people they lead?
- Most businesses need to be taught what servant leadership is about and how it can make a difference. We have somehow convinced ourselves that business and our feelings in business and life should be different and separate, that what works in building relationships in life won't work in a business setting. Leaders must realize that people are people and encouragement, caring, listening, relationships, and sense of community works everywhere.
- Businesses need to establish servant leadership principles and philosophies as a goal for their leaders and then hold them accountable for becoming a servant leader. It cannot be the flavor of the week. It must become a way of life and be sustainable.
- Only people with leadership ability and potential, who clearly understand the leadership expectations for them, should ever be put in leadership positions.
- Businesses must establish the training (teaching), coaching, and mentoring process that helps develop servant leaders. They must remember it is a journey and not an event. The training process must be one that is sustained no matter what is happening in the business.
- Leaders need to embrace servant leadership as something they aspire to become. It should be no different than accountants

who desire to become CPAs or HR professionals who earn their SPHR credentials.

As a reminder, I want to go over who a servant leader is.

## SERVANT LEADERS IN BUSINESS ARE

Men and women who bring their purpose, passion, and character, and when combined with their God-given skills and abilities for leadership, bring out the best in people, helping a business develop and implement a sustainable process for success.

They discovered that people come to work every day with their unique personalities, dreams, goals, skills, and hunger for achieving something bigger than themselves. What they need is the right style of leadership, communication, training, and guidance to help them reach their potential. People don't come to work to fail, produce bad products and services, or have a bad day. It is a leader's responsibility to lead by teaching, encouraging, and helping them discover and reach their potential.

## SERVANT LEADERS BRING A VISION THAT BELIEVES

The best strategy to achieve organizational goals and create competitive advantage is by developing an environment of caring, mutual trust, and respect between the leaders and the people by focusing their efforts and strategy on developing the full potential of all associates and the business, therefore creating a winning partnership.

## SERVANT LEADERS LIVE THEIR VISION BY
- Treating people as the most important asset in the company
- Seeing people not as they are today but their potential
- Realizing people are more important than tasks
- Measuring their own success by the success of those they lead
- Knowing leadership is about building relationships throughout the company
- Impacting people's lives by mentoring and coaching

- Setting goals, objectives, actions, and measurements, with accountability for the results
- Leading not just with their words but with their actions and modeling the behavior
- Believing it is the responsibility of leaders to make a difference in people's lives
- Encouraging, inspiring, and motivating their people

When you see the definition and vision of a servant leader, it seems it should be something every leader and every company would want to embrace. It's hard to argue with developing leaders who exhibit such skills, abilities, vision, and philosophy for leading others. But for many, it's hard for them to understand the importance and make servant leadership a way of life.

Often when companies have tried to start new initiatives to improve relationships with their people, it has failed, because there is no real strategy or plan for developing and implementing a process. Real change takes time, patience and perseverance to make the needed people and culture improvements. They look at it as a program and not as an ongoing process. Programs are usually looked at as something short term, while process-building is for the long term. If servant leadership is going to be successful, leadership must be committed to the journey and the changes that *everyone* in the company will need to make in the way they lead, interact, and think about the people they lead. Some of those changes will require a commitment that causes leaders to learn how to:

- Balance the leadership of the people with the stewardship of the company.
- Establish the expectations with their leadership for this new servant leadership style.
- Obtain support by all senior leadership (from the top), or it will not work
- Ensure leaders, supervisors, and middle -managers who won't support it or cannot change leave the company.
- Realize it is a journey and not a quick fix.
- Communicate the process and the strategy to the total workforce, so they know what is happening and will hold you accountable for making it happen.
- Expect skepticism from some associates.

- Remove the barriers that keep people and the company from reaching their goals.
- Empower your people.
- Dramatically improve communication up and down the chain; communication will be the glue that makes it work.
- Build real relationships with those they lead.
- Make resolving conflict "job one," because there will be plenty of conflicts as you implement this strategy.
- Move your company from reactive to proactive in its personality.
- Position people as problems solvers, not problems in the mind of all the leaders.
- Develop an atmosphere of innovation and imagination.
- Make motivating, encouraging, inspiring, and energizing your people the new normal.
- Train and teach to build your associates into a team of champions.
- See problems as opportunities.
- Concentrate on developing the potential of your people.
- Set goals, objectives, actions, and measurements, with accountability for the results. Build a sense of community, where everyone is pulling together to build your competitive advantage.
- Train, teach, and learn over and over.
- Remember there will sometimes be pain in the journey, but it will be worth it.

Change is never an easy journey. When the implementation of servant leadership principles isn't going as fast or as well as you would like, there will be those who say it isn't going to work. There will be leaders and people who won't catch or support the vision, and they will need to change or move on. As we know, anything worthwhile is never easy. But if your team will truly work together to create a collaborative effort and develop their potential and that of the company, you will create a competitive advantage that will confuse your competitors, as they try and figure out how you are accomplishing your success, how you are beating them in the marketplace, and why your customers love you so much.

As you implement your servant leadership principles, you will begin to see people in a new way, and best of all, you will begin to see a new excitement among your people. Your turnover problems will start to improve, and your vision of becoming the best place in the area to work will become a reality. You will create the security for the workforce and the company that you have always desired. Not only will the smiles of your people become brighter, but the results of your business will begin to improve.

If you can capture this vision for leadership, you will notice a change when you lay your head on your pillow at night and go to sleep. You will start to feel less stress and frustration, knowing you and your company are making a difference in the lives of people. This will give you the true joy and happiness all of us desire: the kind that is achieved by making a difference in the lives of the people God has placed in your path. This is the kind of joy and happiness money, job titles, power and fame can never buy!

Do nothing out of selfish ambition or vain conceit, but in humility consider others better than yourselves.

Philippians 2:3 (NIV)

***God bless you, and enjoy the wonderful journey God has planned for you!***

# Key Lessons Learned
# During My Journey

In this section, I want to go back over the Lessons Learned covered in each chapter. Read and think through each one, using them to help you review your leadership style, what you need to improve on personally, and what steps you need to take to impact the lives of the people God has placed in your path. We only get one shot at this journey called life. Use your talents, skills, and abilities wisely. Make a difference in the lives of the people you do life with. It will bring you great joy, happiness and success as a leader.

## LESSONS LEARNED

Servant leaders are not developed by accident or without a process, plan, purpose, and passion.

Becoming a servant leader requires a personal commitment to keep growing as a leader.

When servant leaders work to help their people become successful, they will do well, and so will the company.

Success is never won on your own; there are many partners.

Every person is gifted with certain talents and skills; it's a leader's role to help him or her discover and reach their potential.

True servant leadership is about sharing life with the people you lead. It's not done successfully stranger to stranger. So build relationships.

Leaders fall because of selfishness and belief in themselves as the ruler of their kingdom.

Be on guard against feeling important and starting to love that feeling.

Your greatest calling as a leader is your family.

Deliver all important messages to your people yourself, or be there when it is given, so you can ensure the right message has been given and is understood.

The types and mix of leadership styles will make a difference in a company's results.

Our people have so much to teach us as leaders about what we were doing wrong and how they could help us fix it. We just need to listen.

Sometimes, God does the unexpected when things are going great to test our faith in him and take us in a different direction and further in our journey than we would go by ourselves.

Sometimes, there is pain in the journey, and it's required to move you to where God wants to bless you.

God is always faithful and can be trusted. Sometimes, you have to go through a storm to find God's purpose for your life and see the awesome rainbows he has prepared for you. I can truly say that I have found many rainbows.

Build trust with your people, and they will move mountains for you.

Success is driven by having the right people, in the right positions, at the right time, doing the right things.

Because they embrace diversity, servant leaders are great team builders. They understand the power of the team. They know that the better a team can work together, the closer they will come to fulfilling their own potential and that of the company.

The people you lead don't expect perfection, but they do expect caring servant leaders who are real and humble.

Servant leaders believe that giving and receiving feedback is the key to building relationships with their people.

Caring about other people's needs and helping them find their potential becomes a good barrier for keeping selfishness out of your own life and teaching you humbleness.

Holding people and a team accountable for the results is one of the strongest tools in a servant leader's toolbox.

What happens to you in life is not as important as your reactions during and after the struggles.

Just imagine what could happen in our companies if we treated our workforce as well as we treated our customers.

Building relationships with your people starts the spark for competitive advantage.

Servant leaders understand that building a strong company starts with each individual, moment by moment.

Start building relationships based on meeting people's needs.

Is a company's biggest people issue they can't find good people, or is it that their process can't keep good people or develop the people who come through the door in the right way?

People on a manufacturing floor know the issues and problems, but many leaders never ask them for their opinion or pay attention to their ideas.

When people fail in their jobs, it is almost always a failure of leadership.

We get the results we allow to happen.

Let people speak their mind, and they will know you appreciate them. Tell them to be quiet or you don't have time to listen, and you will lose them and their value to the organization.

As leaders, we should start with the plank in our own eye before complaining about the speck in someone else's eye.

It's easier to get back up after getting knocked down when people are counting on you than when it is all about you.

I believe that great communication is the main building-block for all our healthy relationships in life and the workplace. Communication can bring a company and its people together as a team, or it can separate them and potentially tear them and the business apart.

Leaders in any organization set the communication style.

Poor and ineffective communication is the number-one problem in business today. It is the root of almost every problem in a business.

Many of the new communication sources—such as e-mail, texting, and voice mail— can make us lazy in our communication if we let them.

Good communication starts on the first day a new associate starts work. Don't do it right, and you are behind the eight ball.

Asking questions and listening are two of the most effective tools in establishing a caring and vibrant workplace.

Servant leaders believe one-on-one meetings and listening to their people are great opportunities for developing understanding.

Listening helps servant leaders understand the differences in their people and their needs, goals, and skills.

Life does not happen without some conflict.

People want to know that the people they are doing life with really care about them.

Servant leaders see the whole person, not just the person who comes and does some work. Servant leaders are in the business of growing people and impacting people's lives.

Servant leaders shine the light on their people's strengths and possibilities and then provide the encouragement and help needed for their people to travel the right path.

The more change that is taking place, the more communication is needed to calm the fire.

No company has ever gone out of business because it didn't produce enough reports or paperwork, but plenty have failed because the communication broke down, and strategy didn't get implemented because the people didn't know.

Show me a vision that is not communicated to the people, and I will show you a company and its people wandering in the desert.

Conference rooms are for private meetings, video conferences, and pizza lunches, not for solving problems or developing people. Go where the people are to find out what is happening.

Real innovation in business is created by not having a fear of failure.

Failure is not meant to be lived alone.

God is involved in all aspects of our lives. Nothing happens to us that God doesn't know about. He is with us during our entire journey. He knows our fears, our scars, doubts, and our imperfections. But he still loves us unconditionally and with all his heart. He brings us grace, mercy, comfort, and hope.

"For God so loved the world that he gave his only begotten Son, that whoever believeth in Him should not perish but have everlasting life" John 3:16 (KJV).

# About the Author

Bill Flint is the founder, president, and CEO of Flint Strategic Partners, a strategic consulting, coaching and leadership training firm located in Goshen, Indiana. During his career, Bill has worked for privately held, mid-sized, and two Fortune 500 companies.

Bill is a disciplined, energetic, and entrepreneurial leader, with thirty-eight years of business experience in the manufacturing sector, with twenty-five of those years in senior leadership positions. His unique combination of real-world business experience, hands-on leadership, and God's blessings has allowed him to realize his long-term dream of starting his own consulting firm and writing a book on servant leadership.

Bill has extensive experience in sales and marketing, having held positions in field sales and as regional sales manager, product manager, sales and marketing manager, and vice president of sales and marketing.

Bill also spent twelve years as president of two manufacturing companies; one with annual sales of $30 million and three manufacturing facilities and another with annual sales of $125 million, eleven hundred associates, and ten manufacturing facilities located in the United States, Mexico, and Europe.

Bill is a member of Nappanee Missionary Church in Nappanee, Indiana, where he serves on the church board, and he and his wife, Kay, teach the newly married Sunday school class. He also serves on the board of directors of Ethos Inc., located in Elkhart, Indiana, and is a member of the Business Advisory Committee for Ivy Tech Community College in South Bend, Indiana; Bill is also a member of The Greater Elkhart Chamber Of

Commerce and The Chamber of Commerce St. Joseph County. Bill is also a certified business adviser with the Organization for Entrepreneurial Development, a nonprofit organization that helps provide support and services for entrepreneurs and leaders in small and mid-sized businesses.

Bill and his wife, Kay, have been married for thirty years, and have lived in Goshen, Indiana, for the last eight years. They have two sons, ages twenty-seven and twenty-nine and two grandsons who, as Bill describes, have given him his favorite title: "Pop Pops."

# The Journey To Competitive Advantage Through Servant Leadership

## Training Process

Our training process is led by our president, Bill Flint, the author of *The Journey to Competitive Advantage through Servant Leadership*. It is an interactive training process developed by Bill to help your senior leadership, middle-management, supervisors, team leaders and future leaders understand the servant leadership philosophy and help them develop the skills, attitude, and abilities needed to maximize the potential of your most important asset: the people who come to work every day.

The training process consists of four modules, each containing five to seven sessions. Each session within a module lasts about two hours, depending on the size of your team and the interaction that takes place. The process also includes (if you desire) individual coaching, individual and team assessments, team-building exercises, and tools to help participants immediately start using what they learn. Because every company is different, our process can be fully customized to fit your budget, timeline, and needs. The training can be delivered at your location, during a weekend retreat, as part of a leadership meeting, or online through our Webinar training process.

You can select the complete, four module training process, choose a specific module, or choose individual sessions that fit into your current training programs. If you would like to receive more information, please call us at 888-395-9054 or e-mail Bill directly at bflint@flintpartners.com.

# The Journey To Competitive Advantage Through Servant Leadership

## Training Modules

### Module 1: Servant Leadership The Competitive Advantage

- How a Servant Leader Can Make a Difference
- Leadership Skills Needed to Gain a Competitive Advantage
- The Five Leadership Styles Found in Every Company
- Converting Servant Leadership into a "Daily Dose"
- Self-Awareness…A Strength of Servant Leaders
- Seven Fundamental Skills of a Servant Leader
- How Poor Leadership Limits an Organization's Potential

### Module 2: Winning Through Communication

- Communication…The Glue
- Conflict Resolution…The Breakfast of Champions
- The Art of Inspiring Others
- Dealing with Difficult People
- Fifteen Ways to Mess Up Morale

### Module 3: Jump-Start Your Strategy

- Breathing Life into Your Company's Mission and Vision
- Discovering and Eliminating the Pain in Your Organization

- Creating and Implementing Transformational Strategies
- Execute Beyond Your Wildest Dreams

## Module 4: Leading and Building Your Team

- Motivation Starts with Discovering the Needs of Your People
- Building Successful Relationships with Your Team
- Build Strong Leaders Through Coaching and Mentoring
- Developing Winners at All Levels of the Organization
- Moving Average Team Members to Excellent Performers

## Training Process, Seminars, Consulting, Coaching, and Speaking Engagements

If you would like more information on our servant leadership training process, consulting services, coaching, seminars, retreats, webinars, speaking engagements, or to receive our free newsletter and purchase books for your leadership team **CONTACT US**:

Flint Strategic Partners
57670 Boulder Court
Goshen, IN 46528
Attention: Bill Flint
E-mail: bflint@flintpartners.com
Website: www.flintpartners.com
Website: www.servantleaders.org (Book and training information)
Blog: flintstrategicpartners.blogspot.com/
Twitter: @FlintPartners
Phone: 888-395-9054

*Discounts are available on book purchases in quantities of ten or more.

*Discounts are available on all services and purchases of our book by church groups, nonprofits, civic organizations, and institutions of higher learning.